ROUTLEDGE LIBRARY EDITIONS:
AID

Volume 4

U.S. ECONOMIC FOREIGN AID

U.S. ECONOMIC FOREIGN AID

A Case Study of the United States Agency for International Development

DAVID PORTER

Routledge
Taylor & Francis Group
LONDON AND NEW YORK

First published in 1990 by Garland Publishing Inc.

This edition first published in 2020
by Routledge
2 Park Square, Milton Park, Abingdon, Oxon OX14 4RN

and by Routledge
52 Vanderbilt Avenue, New York, NY 10017

Routledge is an imprint of the Taylor & Francis Group, an informa business

British Library Cataloguing in Publication Data
A catalogue record for this book is available from the British Library

ISBN: 978-0-367-27806-9 (Set)
ISBN: 978-0-429-32859-6 (Set) (ebk)
ISBN: 978-0-367-34878-6 (Volume 4) (hbk)
ISBN: 978-0-429-32858-9 (Volume 4) (ebk)

Publisher's Note
The publisher has gone to great lengths to ensure the quality of this reprint but points out that some imperfections in the original copies may be apparent.

Disclaimer
The publisher has made every effort to trace copyright holders and would welcome correspondence from those they have been unable to trace.

FOREIGN ECONOMIC POLICY OF THE UNITED STATES

U.S. Economic Foreign Aid

A Case Study of the United States Agency for International Development

DAVID PORTER

GARLAND PUBLISHING, INC.
NEW YORK & LONDON • 1990

Library of Congress Cataloging-in-Publication Data

Porter, David (David Stanley)
U.S. economic foreign aid: a case study of the United States Agency for International Development/ David Porter.
p. cm.—(Foreign economic policy of the United States)
Includes bibliographical references.
ISBN 0-8240-7466-1 (alk. paper)
1. Economic assistance, American. 2. United States. Agency for International Development. I. Title. I. Series.
HC60.P59 1990
353.0089—dc20 90-3612

Printed on acid-free, 250-year-life paper.
Manufactured in the United States of America

TABLE OF CONTENTS

TABLE OF CONTENTS

LIST OF TABLES

LIST OF TABLES

LIST OF TABLES

LIST OF FIGURES

PREFACE

The research being presented is part of an ongoing research project concerning the allocation of United States bilateral economic foreign aid administered by the Agency for International Development (AID). Originally the project was limited to a doctoral dissertation that was primarily concerned with replicating the research of Kato, McKinlay and Little, and other empirical researchers in the field of United States bilateral foreign aid allocations. The dissertation left several question unanswered, however, and research has continued unabated.

Like the research completed for the doctoral dissertation, the research being reported here studies the allocation of United States bilateral foreign aid for the years 1968-1976. The differences is that this project addresses earlier criticisms and methodological issues, such as the use of percapita measures, and the data base has been expanded and improved. While this research is clearly an expansion and extension of the earlier research the basic conclusions have remained unchanged. This means that at least four independent researchers using different data bases, and employing various empirical research techniques have reached basically the same conclusions.

When the empirical foreign aid research is combined and viewed as a continuous body of knowledge one is provided with a comprehensive study of foreign aid allocation from 1961 through 1983. Based on this body of research it appears clear that foreign aid is utilized as a tool of foreign policy by the United States, and the allocation pattern for all forms of foreign aid reflects the national self interest of the United States. Thus through replication reliability is increased and our understanding of US foreign aid policy is significantly enhanced. (see Chapters Two and Three)

While the basic patterns and causes of foreign aid allocations have been identified, there remains a need for additional research in the field for three reasons. First, foreign aid presents an excellent opportunity to investigate a number of theoretical issues in comparative politics, international relations, domestic institutional decision making, and the development of political and economic institutions.

Preface

To test the eight foreign aid models operationalized for this study it was necessary to measure poverty, the level of democratic development, economic growth, military alliances, systemic stability, the influence of agricultural and other interest groups on Congressional decision making, the relationship between Congress and the President and the relative institutional strength of AID in relation to several other institutions that influence United States foreign policy and foreign aid allocations. Primarily as a result of the difficulties in encountered in specifying the basic human needs model, a major emphasis of the research project has been the development of a theoretically consistent measure of poverty. With the development of better indicators and measures our understanding of foreign aid policy will be expanded, and will make contributions to related fields of research.

The second reason for continuing research in the field of foreign aid is that the United States is only one of several actors in the international transferer of foreign aid funds. One basic question is whether the United States allocation pattern is representative of the foreign aid policies of other donor states. A second question is the relationship between bilateral foreign aid and multilateral foreign aid.

As part of the research project the allocation of United States bilateral foreign aid, administered by AID, has been compared with the with multinational aid distribution patterns. The analysis was limited to Latin America but the results were informative and have been published. Later the multi and bilateral analysis will be expanded to include Africa and Asia. After considering the three regions independently, cross regional comparisons will be made.

The final reason for continuing foreign aid research is that as a tool of foreign policy, one must ask the question of what happens to the pattern of allocations when foreign policy changes? Historically, there is reason to believe that as foreign policy priorities change allocation patterns change. Given the events of 1989 and 1990, and the apparent decline or end of the cold war one would expect foreign aid pattern to change during the 1990s. The interesting question is whether they will change to reflect some altruistic objectives, or will foreign aid continue to reflect the short term foreign policy interests of the donor state?

INTRODUCTION

> "of all the seeming and real innovations which the modern age has introduced into the practice of foreign policy none has proven more baffling to both understanding and action than foreign aid"
>
> (Morgenthau:62:301)

Currently, there are two basic approaches to explaining the foreign aid policy of the United States; the international approach, and the domestic approach. There are several basic similarities between the two approaches; however, they vary in one key aspect. The international approach utilizes the nation state as the unit of analysis; while the second approach, the domestic approach, adopts intra-state, or domestic, institutions as the unit of analysis.

The international approach attempts to explain the distribution of United States foreign aid across recipient states by examining relationships that are external to the donor state. This body of research utilizes the nation state as the unit of analysis, and explains the allocation of scarce foreign aid funds by examining the bilateral relations between the donor and recipient states. This approach derives its theoretical premises from the field of international relations.

The second approach explains United States foreign aid policy by examining the intrastate, or domestic institutions, of the donor state. This approach explains United States foreign aid policy by examining the characteristics and interactions between domestic institutions that have decision making authority over foreign aid policy. In addition, the domestic approach has specified decision making strategies for each domestic institution based on specified salient characteristics, including constitutional-legal authority, organizational goals, and strategic premises. This approach derives its theoretical justifications from the decision making theories of the public administration field.

Both approaches have their strengths and weaknesses. The international approach has been successful in specifying a number of empirical models that capture various foreign aid objectives of the donor state. Through regression analysis these models have been successfully tested, and while there remains specification and methodological problems, the international approach has been able to explain a significant portion of United States foreign aid allocations across recipient states. However, by focusing on the nation state as the unit of analysis any potential variance across domestic institutions in their foreign aid policy objectives, organizational goals, outside domestic influences, or other decision making determinants, at the sub-national level, are suppressed.

The domestic approach has been successful in identifying significant variances between institutions that have substantive legal authority over foreign aid decisions. More specifically, the decision making strategies of institutions vary in their environmental constraints, organizational goals, and in the political relationships that influence the foreign aid policy of the United States. While the domestic approach has been successful in identifying the institutional characteristics and relationships that influence foreign aid policy, they have not been able to explain why a specific recipient state receives a given level of foreign aid; nor have they been able to operationalize their descriptive research into empirical models capable of supporting or falsifying the hypothesized causes of foreign aid policy.

Both the international and domestic approaches to explaining the foreign aid policy of the United States can be strengthened by applying the international empirical models of aid distribution to explain the decision making process of domestic institutions. By employing empirical models of aid distribution at the domestic level the hypotheses found in the domestic literature can be tested, while simultaneously our understanding of foreign aid allocations across recipient states will be expanded. This is the primary research objective of this study.

To achieve this research objective, this analysis is organized into five chapters. The first chapter provides a historical review of the United States foreign aid program that identifies important historical characteristics which help to define the temporal period of this study. The second chapter will international literature, while the third chapter considers the domestic literature. The fourth chapter specifies an analytical framework that is theoretically consistent with the rational choice paradigm. The empirical models, variables, and indicators will be outlined in this chapter. The final chapter, the fifth, will report the empirical findings and present conclusions based on empirical outcomes.

CHAPTER ONE

THE HISTORICAL DEVELOPMENT OF UNITED STATES FOREIGN AID POLICY

> "In the history of Diplomacy, subsidies and tributes have been common ... but the peace time economic aid among governments is novel"
>
> (Ohlin:66:9)

Throughout World War II, the United States provided foreign aid in the form of war materials and economic credits to assist its allies in the war effort. (Black:68:4-12) In the closing days of World War II, the United States had to decide whether to continue the systematic transfer of wealth to other nations or to discontinue the policy of assistance as was the case at the end of World War I. The decision to continue providing assistance began a new era in the relations between rich and poor nations, and marked the first time the United States adopted a policy of systematic and annual transfer of substantial economic resources to other countries during peacetime.

The History of US Foreign Aid Policy

This decision in 1945, to continue to provide assistance after victory, marked the beginning of the modern foreign aid policy era. (Holbert:66:20) Since that time, the United States' foreign aid policy has gone through three distinct periods, each with its own enabling legislation, policy mandates, political priorities, and administrating agencies. (see Figure One)

THE FIRST FOREIGN AID PERIOD

The first period began with the close of World War II and ends with the National Security Act of 1951. (Pastor:80:256) Immediately after the war, the greatest need was for simple relief including; housing, food, medication, and resettlement. At first, the peacetime aid policies designed to meet these needs were simply extensions of wartime programs, such as Lend-Lease and the UNRRA. The principle recipients, during this period, were Western European. (Black:68:4-5)

However, as the political-economic problems of the post-World War II era, and the politics of the Cold War, began to develop the need for a more comprehensive policy to provide for the reconstruction and the recovery of Western Europe became apparent. The response was the establishment of the Marshall Plan in March of 1948. The dominant forms of aid during this period were economic grants and loans with only a relatively small portion of total aid expenditures going to military assistance. (Pastor:80:256)

THE SECOND FOREIGN AID PERIOD

The second period is dominated by its enabling legislation, the Mutual Security Act of 1951, and as the name of the enabling legislation suggests, the paramount objective of foreign aid during the second period was the security of the United States and its allies. The political goal of the Mutual Security Act of 1951 was consistent with the general emphasis of United States foreign policy at the time, which stressed the containment of Communism. The Act itself was partly a response to the Korean War which created concern over the defensive capabilities of United States and its allies. To contain Communism the United States began to allocate foreign assistance to our allies on the rim of the Soviet Union. (Pastor:80:256-266)

Prior to this time, the primary emphasis in United States foreign aid policy was economic, but the new security concerns of the United States quickly shifted foreign aid priorities from economic aid to military assistance. During the first period the ratio of economic to military aid was 4:1, by 1954 the ratio had reversed itself; for every dollar allocated for economic aid the United States was allocating four dollars for military aid. (Pastor:80:256)

The different periods of United States foreign aid overlap and the enabling legislation of one period has often been based on earlier, though less comprehensive legislation. At first, aid for the recovery of Europe was an extension of wartime programs and policies. The Mutual Security Act was based on antecedent legislation including military aid to Greece and Turkey, the Philippines Military Assistance Act, and NATO. It's important to note that throughout the post-World War II period United States foreign aid has included both military and economic assistance.

The distinguishing factor between the three periods is the emphasis of one form of aid over the other, the administrating agencies, and the legal constraints and policy objectives of the enabling legislation. Under the Mutual Security Act, for example, the United States had a mutual security obligation as a condition for economic assistance. As a consequence one would expect the allocations of United States bilateral aid to reflect United States security requirements and commitments. And, it appears reasonable to assume, that the differences in legal authorizations, policy mandates, administrating agencies, and other variables between the three periods will effect the distribution of United States economic aid for their perspective periods. (Mason:64:41)

THE THIRD FOREIGN AID PERIOD

The third period of United States foreign aid policy is dominated by the concept of aid to promote economic development, or developmental assistance. The allocation of aid for development and has its origins in Point IV of President Truman's 1949 inaugural address:

> "The policy of the United States is to aid the efforts of the peoples economically underdeveloped areas to develop their resources and improve living conditions."
>
> President Truman, Inaugural Address, Point IV, 1949

When President Truman announced this ambitious policy in 1949, its symbolism was more impressive than its substantive impact on foreign aid policy. The budget request for foreign aid in the 1949 fiscal year included some seven billion dollars for the Marshall Plan and related programs for the recovery of Europe, and only forty-five million dollars for Point IV countries. (Pastor:80:269) Point IV, nevertheless, did establish development aid as a national policy for the United States. But, twelve years would pass before development aid became the paramount priority of the United States foreign aid policy.

President Truman's Point IV policy, and development aid, is not necessarily a question of military versus economic assistance. There are respected theories of economic development that predict periods of political instability caused by the rising demands and expectations that are a natural result of economic development. (Huntington:68:1-88) Under these conditions, the distribution of military aid might conceivably be necessary to restore political stability and insure continued economic development. Development aid is basically a question of distribution priorities.

The first period was dominated by distribution of United States bilateral aid to Western Europe, the second foreign aid period by distribution to countries on the rim of the Soviet Union. (Pastor:80:256) The third period of United States foreign aid policy is dominated by aid policies and legal authorizations designed to assist the less developed regions of the world in their economic development.

(Nelson:68:14-19)(see Figure One) And, the observable distribution pattern for the third period is dominated by the allocation of economic assistance to the less developed, the poor countries, of the international system. It is this distribution pattern that separates the third foreign aid period from the two previous periods.

There are several reasons why development aid did not dominate early United States foreign aid policy. First, is the economic condition of Europe which mandated that recovery and reconstruction consume the majority of scarce foreign aid expenditures. Point IV could conceivable have been implemented after the reconstruction of Europe and one could argue that this was the original intent of President Truman. However, just as such a transition became feasible, the United States became preoccupied, if not besieged, with security concerns caused by the loss of China, the Korean War, the increased Soviet threat in Europe and the beginnings of the Indo-China War.

Finally, it must be remembered that during the 1940s and the 1950s, the first two periods of United States foreign aid policies, most of the undeveloped regions of the world were colonies of European states. A rationale for a type of international division of responsibility developed whereby each colonial power was responsible for providing aid to its former colonies. (Mason:64:72-81) As a consequence, all of Africa and a substantial portion of Asia, outside the Philippines Islands, were considered ineligible for United States development aid. The United States primary responsibility during this period was to assist in the development of Latin America, and what development aid was provided from 1949 through 1959 tended to be concentrated in this region. (Mason:64:72-81) The primary program for providing assistance to the less developed regions of the world during this period was PL 480, the Food for Peace Program, which was "admittedly devised less for the concern for the developing world than from a domestic problem" of a large surplus of farm commodities. (Pastor:80:269)

President Truman in his 1949 Inaugural Address adopted development aid as a formal policy of the United States, twelve years later in his Inaugural Address, President Kennedy reaffirmed the Point IV policy and specified development aid as the paramount principle of United States foreign aid policy.

> "To those people in the huts and villages of half the globe struggling to break the bonds of mass misery, we pledge our best efforts to help them help themselves, for whatever period

> is required, not because the Communist may be doing it, not because we seek their votes, but because it is right. If a free society cannot help the many who are poor, it cannot save the few who are rich."
>
> President Kennedy Inaugural Address, January, 1961

President Kennedy operationalized his policy declaration by requesting Congress to replace the ten year old Mutual Security Act with new enabling legislation that became the Foreign Assistance Act of 1961. (Nelson:68:1-14) Under the new enabling legislation there can be no question that the distribution of United States foreign aid shifted from the nations on the rim of the Soviet Union to the developing nations of the international system.

To some extent the shift in distributional patterns began in the late 1950s as the United States responded to increased demands from the new nations that were emerging from decolonization. (Little & Clifford:65:17) However, whether developmental foreign aid administered under the new act was distributed to meet the demands of the new states, or in response to United States foreign policy objectives, such as national security, or economic self interest, has been a major focus of debate in the foreign aid literature.

A second impact of the Kennedy policy initiative was a comprehensive revamping of the administrative agencies responsible for carrying out United States foreign aid policy. Prior to 1961 the foreign aid policy of the United States was administered by a number of often changing and poorly coordinated agencies. The inefficiencies of the administrative system were widely acknowledged and several evaluative reports including the Gray Report, Partners in Progress Report, and The Administration of Foreign Affairs Report recommended the establishment of one central coordinating agency which would have primary responsibilities for implementation, coordination and administration of policy. (Brown & Opie:53:506-508)

President Kennedy's developmental emphasis included the restructuring of the aid administrative network through the creation the Agency for International Development (A.I.D.). A.I.D. subsequently became the central coordinating agency for all bilateral United States economic aid and for certain types of supportive military aid. (Black:68:6-7) Direct military aid in the form of arm sales and assistance, and training military personnel, though coordinated by A.I.D., remain under the jurisdiction, budget authority, and responsibility of the Department of Defense. (Black:68:6-7)

The use of overlapping and changing administrative agencies prior to the establishment of A.I.D. has an important impact on the temporal period of this study. Both the international and domestic approaches to explaining United States foreign aid policy develop decision making models derived from the rational choice paradigm. To apply the rational choice paradigm to an organization, regardless whether one's level of analysis is the nation state or domestic institution, certain minimum theoretical standards must be met; including some minimum level of variance in environmental constraints, legal authority, political relationships, and the organizational structure of the decision making units of interest.

At the nation state level of analysis the discrepancies of organizational structure and legal authority between A.I.D. and its predecessor agencies is relatively unimportant. However, when the level of analysis is reduced to explaining the behavior of domestic institutions, with substantive legal authority over United States foreign aid policy, the variance between A.I.D. and its predecessor agencies becomes a significant challenge to validity. Of particular concern is the tendency to fragmentize the administrative responsibilities and reporting systems of administering agencies prior to 1961.

The Mutual Security Agency, for example, reported directly to the President; while the Technical Cooperation Administration was an autonomous unit within the Department of State, the International Cooperation Administration was a semi-autonomous agency within the same cabinet department, and the Development Loan Fund was an independent government corporation. With the passage of the Foreign Assistance Act of 1961 these functions were merged into a single autonomous agency, A.I.D., and placed under the offices of the State Department. (Black:68:3-11) (see Figure Two)

The three foreign aid periods reviewed vary in their enabling legislation, policy mandates, and administrating agencies. Some researchers, such as Pastor, hypothesize that the basic human needs amendments of 1973 mark a fourth foreign aid period. The hypothesized fourth foreign aid period varies from the earlier three periods in that the "thrust of [the United States] bilateral development program changed from an economic strategy of maximizing gross national product, . . . to a more socially oriented strategy of helping the poorest countries and the poorest sectors of the population in those countries". (Pastor:80:278) Unlike the three earlier foreign aid periods, the policy mandate of the basic human needs amendments of 1973 did not establish new foreign aid agencies, or mandate additional foreign policy programs.

The 1973 legislation amended, but did not replace the enabling legislation of 1961, and A.I.D.'s budgetary categories and program activity reports submitted to Congress in 1972, are organized and contain the same basic information as A.I.D.'s reports of 1974, and 1976. In addition it is questionable whether A.I.D.'s political relationships within the executive branch, particularly in regards to the Departments of State, Treasury, and Agriculture, were significantly altered by the 1973 amendments to the Foreign Assistance Act. (see Chapter Three more a more detailed discussion) Consequently, whether the alteration of A.I.D.'s policy mandate in 1973 caused a substantive change in the allocation pattern of bilateral economic aid administered by A.I.D. is questionable, and is a matter for empirical investigation. Whether the 1973 basic human needs amendments significantly effected United States foreign aid allocations is a secondary research question, which will be empirically tested.

THE TEMPORAL PERIOD

To control for the potential variance in foreign aid policy decisions caused by the variances in organizational structure, legal authority, political relationships, and other differences between A.I.D. and its predecessor agencies presents substantial theoretical and data difficulties, which are unnecessary to the primary research objective. These difficulties can be avoided through the adoption of research parameters pertaining to the temporal period. This study will concentrate its analysis on explaining the foreign aid policy of the United States as administered under the Foreign Assistance act of 1961, as amended, by the Agency for International Development (A.I.D.).

Since the establishment of A.I.D. the international system, the foreign and domestic politics of the United States, and the policy mandates of A.I.D have changed significantly. Hypothetically, one would expect the allocation of United States bilateral foreign aid to reflect these changes; and ideally the temporal period should encompass the entire third foreign aid period, from 1961 through 1985. Unfortunately a twenty-four year temporal period significantly increases the complexities of the research project to the point where the disadvantages out weigh the advantages.

To test the ten hypotheses proposed in Chapter Four requires the operationalization of three dependent variables and some sixty independent variables for each year of the temporal period. Collecting this amount of data from the early 1960s through the mid 1980s significantly increases methodological complexities and raises questions of theoretical consistency. To insure theoretical consistency data sources must be compatible over the temporal period. To collect data over twenty-four years would require the use of multiple data sources per indicator, which raises questions of consistent measures. While this problem is not insurmountable, it unnecessarily increases the complexities of the research project. The primary research objective is the test for any significant variance between the Executive and Congress in the foreign aid decision making process. To achieve this goal it is unnecessary to test the entire twenty-four year period.

To meet the primary research objective and to measure any potential variance caused by changes in the international system, the foreign and domestic politics of the United States, and the changes in A.I.D.'s policy mandate, it is necessary that three conditions be met.

First, to provide comparison with the research of others, the temporal period must over lap with previous empirical research on foreign aid. Second, the temporal period must capture the potential effects of the Vietnam War. And third, the temporal period needs to capture the effects of the basic human needs and human rights allocation criteria adopted in the early 1970s. These goals can be achieved with a temporal period that begins in the mid 1960s and ends in the mid 1970s, consequently the temporal period adopted for this research is the nine year period 1967-1975. It is assumed that the allocation of foreign aid during year one is based on the events and conditions of the previous year. Consequently, the temporal period is inclusive of the fiscal years 1968-1976.

FIGURE ONE

POST WORLD WAR TWO FOREIGN AID PERIODS

YEAR	PRIMARY ENABLING LEGISLATION	PRIMARY DISTRIBUTION PATTERN
1945-1951	MARSHALL PLAN 1948	WESTERN EUROPE
1951-1961	MUTUAL SECURITY ACT 1951 FOOD FOR PEACE 1954	COUNTRIES ON THE RIM OF THE USSR
1961-PRESENT	FOOD FOR PEACE CONT. FOREIGN ASSISTANCE ACT 1961	POOR, OR THE LESS DEVELOPED COUNTRIES
NEW PERIOD 1973-PRESENT	BASIC HUMAN NEEDS AMENDMENTS 1973	THE POOREST OF THE POOR

(Pastor:80:256-266)

FIGURE TWO

A PARTIAL LIST OF US FOREIGN AID AGENCIES

AGENCY	TIME PERIOD	STATUS IN EX. BRANCH
ECONOMIC CO-OPERATION ADMINISTRATION	1948-1952	CABINET STATUS
MUTUAL SECURITY AGENCY	1951-1953	EXECUTIVE OFFICE UNDER PRESIDENT
FOREIGN OPERATION ADMINISTRATION	1953-1955	DIRECTOR WAS MEMBER OF CABINET
INTERNATIONAL CO-OPERATION ADMIN.	1955-1961	SEMIAUTONOMOUS AGENCY UNDER STATE DEPARTMENT
DEVELOPMENT LOAN FUND	1955-1961	INDEPENDENT AGENCY
AGENCY FOR INTERNATIONAL DEVELOPMENT (AID)	1961 TO PRESENT	SEMIAUTONOMOUS AGENCY UNDER THE STATE DEPT.

(Cunnungham:74:69)

CHAPTER TWO

THE INTERNATIONAL EXPLANATIONS OF FOREIGN AID POLICY

> "Aid means the transfer of resources from the government or citizens of one country to those of another, on terms that, from the point of view of the receiver are easier than could be obtained on the capital market" (Mason:64:12)

The international approach usually assumes that foreign aid is "an economic instrument of foreign policy." (Liska:63:62) As an instrument of foreign policy, foreign aid is used to pursue those interests that cannot be achieved through military or diplomatic means alone. (Morgenthau:62:301) To illustrate the importance of foreign aid as a tool of foreign policy Nelson noted that in "many countries it [foreign aid] is the primary instrument relied upon to protect and promote central United States interests." (Nelson:68:1)

The classification of economic assistance as an instrument of foreign policy has a substantive impact on the specification of foreign aid policy models. Foreign policy is defined as an act beyond the boundaries of the nation state that is directed toward another international actor; in the case of foreign aid the second actor is the recipient state. It is assumed that foreign policy acts are an expression of national self interests. (Holsti:83 :19 & 97-121) By classifying foreign aid as an economic instrument of the donor state's foreign policy, the assumption of national self interest is extended to include foreign aid policies. Consequently the foreign policy explanation assumes that the distribution of foreign aid is determined by the self interest of the donor state. (Mason:64:107)

This classification of assistance as an economic instrument of foreign policy is not universally accepted. Those who challenge or reject the foreign policy assumption stress the formal developmental goals of A.I.D. and the policy objectives articulated by various presidents, including the inaugural addresses of Truman and Kennedy, which stress the humanitarian and developmental objectives of United States foreign aid policy.

The humanitarian explanation adopts normative values by stressing the moral obligation of rich nations towards the less fortunate peoples of the world, and conceptualizes aid as a type of international welfare policy, or transfer of wealth. (Streeten:75:basic premise of book) Rather than basing aid distribution on the foreign policy objectives of the donor state, this explanation stresses that the "United States agency allocating developmental funds should not have to consider anything beyond the technical criteria which have been established." (Ohlin:69:32)*

The two explanations are not necessarily mutually exclusive. It is feasible that some portion of United States aid is distributed for reasons of foreign policy while other forms of assistance are distributed for humanitarian purposes. However, the two explanations are distinct in that they presume significantly different motives and policy objectives to explain foreign aid decisions and allocations. Because of the variance in policy objectives, the predicted pattern of foreign aid allocations vary substantially.

---

* Humanitarian aid is an act beyond the boundaries of the donor state, but is not classified as foreign policy because the donor self interest assumption is violated. To avoid confusion the use of the term foreign policy is limited to those acts that are classified as being in the interest of the donor state.

International Explanations

The foreign policy explanation predicts a distribution pattern based on the self interest of the donor state with the level of assistance allocated to any given recipient state being depended upon the recipient state's utility in reference to the donor state's foreign policy. The humanitarian model, in contrast, predicts that foreign aid allocations will be based on the relative need of the recipient state. The distribution of bilateral aid based on the level of human need is sometimes referred to as aid to the poorest of the poor. Both the foreign policy and humanitarian explanations have been operationalized as empirical models and statistically tested. However, since they are basically competing explanations representing an "an idealistic and materialistic view of aid," they will be considered separately, as independent explanations. (Liska:63:26)

The review of the foreign aid literature, will start with the foreign policy explanation, followed by consideration of the recipient interest, or humanitarian explanation. Each section reviews the descriptive literature, and concludes with the empirical research. However, to avoid repetition it is appropriate to begin with a brief consideration of the common elements of the empirical literature. After which the literature will be divided into seven specific foreign aid decision-making strategies: six derived from the foreign policy explanation, and one derived from the recipient need explanation.

THE EMPIRICAL RESEARCH

> "To the extent that the annual fund for aid is limited and there are many nations in need of aid, the allocation of aid is analogous to the allocation of scarce resources among several alternatives". (KATO:69:199)

The empirical research can be divided into two broad classifications; the first group provides a limited analysis by focusing on one model, or strategy to explain the allocation of United States bilateral foreign aid. The second group is more comprehensive, in the sense that they operationalized several models and test competing explanations. There are significant variances between the two groups, however they share a common theoretical and methodological approach, which makes cross comparisons theoretically feasible and appropriate. Both classifications adopt the rational choice paradigm as the primary analytical tool used to operationalize decision making models and test the hypothesized causal relationship.

International Explanations

Most of the empirical research is limited to the consideration of only one foreign aid model, or strategy. Mosley, Hoadley, Cohn and Wood, for example, consider the relationship between basic human need and the allocation of United States bilateral aid, and Schoultz considers the effects of the Carter Administration's human rights policy on the allocation of bilateral foreign aid. While the findings of these researchers are informative, this research project adopts a more comprehensive approach. Consequently, there will be a tendency to focus on the second group of researchers.

The more comprehensive empirical studies of the allocation of United States bilateral foreign aid have been published by Kato, and two researchers working in collaboration, McKinlay and Little. Kato, and McKinlay and Little adopt the same basic research design to explain the allocation of bilateral foreign aid; including the adoption of the donor state as the decision maker of interest, specifying several sets of distinct independent variables designed to capture different propositions, and specifying expenditures as the dependent variable. To test their propositions and hypothesized relationships, Kato and McKinlay and Little utilize multiple regression analysis and ordinary least squares statistical techniques to measure and compare the relative validity of the foreign aid decision making models operationalized.

Still there are significant variances between Kato's and McKinlay and Little's research in relation to the empirical models operationalized, the selection of indications, and in their experimental design. Do to these differences in research design and theoretical parameters a direct comparison of Kato's and Mckinlay and Little's empirical findings is informative but not necessarily conclusive.

For example, while the empirical findings of both researchers support the foreign policy explanation, Kato does not operationalize a model derived from the recipient need explanation; consequently there can be no comparison of the relative explanatory power of the two competiting explanations based on Kato's research. Also Kato provides a comparison of military and economic aid and concludes that there are significant variances in distribution patterns, suggesting that the two forms of aid a used to achieve varying policies objectives. (Kato:69) McKinlay and Little in contrast operationalize the Recipient Need model but do not test for any potential variance across foreign aid programs. (McKinlay and Little:77 & 79)

International Explanations

Kato operationalized five models to explain the allocation of United States bilateral aid. (Kato:69:201-202) (see Figure Four) Each model is regressed against three dependent variables, military aid, economic aid, and general aid, or total foreign aid commitments. The results of Kato's analysis justifies the independent consideration of military and economic foreign aid. The regression coefficient R squared for military aid was .4906 and .1206 for economic aid. (Kato:69:207)

Kato's results indicate that military foreign aid decisions utilize a significantly different ranking of policy preferences in comparison to economic foreign aid decisions. (Kato:69:207-213)(see Figure Five) Kato compared the relative salience of security variables in relation to military and economic foreign aid and concluded that "the salience of alliance and threat variables shifts from a high to low level as we move from military aid to economic aid." (Kato:69:207) Kato reached similar conclusions in relation to economic variables; "the trade variable is more important in economic aid" and "that the sign of the coefficient in the balance of payments variable is positive in military and negative in economic aid" and finally Kato found that "domestic economic variables have a greater impact on economic aid than on military aid". (Kato:69:207) (see Figure Five)

International Explanations

Kato's analysis of the variance between military and economic foreign aid indicates that the donor state emphasizes different rank order criteria in the allocation of the two forms of foreign aid. This is the primary strength and contribution of Kato's research. There are two primary weaknesses of Kato's research.

First is his failure to operationalize the humanitarian foreign aid explanation, and his consideration of the foreign policy explanation is not exhaustive. Consequently his analysis is incomplete. The second weakness is the short temporal period, 1961-1964. The length of the temporal period does not permit adequate comparison of annual allocation decisions, nor can one speculate concerning potential changes in the donor state's foreign aid priorities over time. In contrast to Kato's research, McKinlay and Little consider the allocation of total United States foreign aid over a ten year period (1960-70), and found that the allocation varied over time. (McKinlay and Little:79:249-250)

Kato's research is unique in its consideration of domestic economic influences. No other empirical work considered for this research project adopts an empirical domestic economic model. Kato's findings are mixed, the domestic model is reported as having "a greater impact on economic aid than on military aid", but apparently the salience of the model is limited. (Kato:69:207) Specific measures are not reported, but Kato's findings are an indication that the level of the deficit and the aid program budget as a proportion of GNP, are considerations in the allocation of United States bilateral foreign aid. (Kato:69:202)

Kato's research was one of the first empirical efforts to explain comprehensively United States bilateral foreign aid allocations and subsequent researcher's both acknowledge and extend Kato's research. McKinlay and Little, for example, acknowledge some of the resemblances between their research and Kato's, but they also note that their research; 1) uses a larger population, 2) has a longer temporal period, and 3) utilizes a more comprehensive array of independent variables. (McKinlay and Little:79:238: Footnote number nine)

McKinlay and Little have published two works analyzing the allocation of United States foreign aid, the first in 1977 and the second in 1979. However, the 1979 research is primarily a refinement of their 1977 research. Consequently, the consideration of McKinlay and Little's research will focus on their 1979 article "The United States Aid Relationship: A Test of the Recipient Need and Donor Interest Models."

McKinlay and Little specify two substantive models of aid allocation, the Recipient Need model which captures the humanitarian explanation, and the Donor Interest model which captures the foreign policy explanation. For the Recipient Need model, McKinlay and Little operationalize indicators that measure the poverty of the recipient state in relation to both national income and basic human need. It is hypothesized that the amount of aid allocated is proportional to the recipient state's need. The Donor Interest model is operationalized as five submodels designed to capture the various foreign policy goals of the donor state. (McKinlay and Little:79:240-243) (see Figure Six)

Each of the models operationalized by McKinlay and Little, and the other empirical researchers, requires a theoretical justification before they can be operationalized and tested. Before considering the findings of the empirical research it is necessary to review these justifications in depth; beginning with the foreign policy explanations.

International Explanations

THE FOREIGN POLICY EXPLANATIONS OF FOREIGN AID POLICY

> "The objective of modern foreign aid . . . is to create a condition that would induce or consolidate a relationship which in turn would generate desirable results."
>
> (Kiska:63:62)

Foreign aid, as a tool of foreign policy, represents a political act by the donor state directed toward the recipient state. As a consequence the foreign policy explanation defines all forms of assistance as being political with only pure humanitarian aid a being per-se non-political. (Morgenthau:62:301) As a political instrument of foreign policy, foreign aid can be used to bolster anti-communist regimes, influence elections to favor pro-American candidates, and to promote anti-communist foreign policies on the part of the recipient state. (Nelson:68:19-27)

For example, aid was used to influence recipient state votes on the admission of the Peoples Republic of China to the United Nations. (Black:68:19) And, foreign aid was used to influence the domestic policies and the formation of governing institutions in the Dominican Republic after the fall of Rafael Trujillo in 1961. (Lowenthal:65) Foreign aid can be used to promote the general goodwill or to influence specific political acts as a prior condition. (Morgenthau:62:301)

These are examples of specific political acts that represent and illustrate the application of more generalized policies and decision making strategies. The main focus of this research project is not to examine or explain specific foreign aid acts or tactics. Rather it is to examine the decision making strategies which cause the more specific application of policy. This requires the identification and specification of policy objectives which cause the foreign aid decisions of the donor state, and result in the observable distribution patterns of foreign aid allocations.

One determining element has already been identified. The third foreign aid period, which runs from 1961 to the present, is dominated by the concept of aid to assist poor countries in their economic development. Consequently, the research task is to explain the distribution of United States bilateral economic assistance across the poor, or developing, states of the international system.

International Explanations

The transfer of economic wealth to poor states is an illustration of the United States' central interest in promoting economic development. However, the United States is more interested in the economic development of certain states than in the development of other states. (Little & Clifford:65:93) These relative developmental interests are reflected in the pattern of United States bilateral foreign aid allocations. To explain these allocations it is necessary is to identify the causal agents that explain why the United States is more interested in promoting the economic development of certain third world states and is less interested in the development of other third world states.

The foreign policy explanation can be tested by specifying empirical models that capture the various foreign policy objectives of the donor state. According to Little and Clifford, there are three basic foreign policy objectives that can be achieved or enhanced through the transfer of economic resources. They include commercial or economic interests, political interests, and national security interests. (Little & Clifford: 65:79) Each of these policy objectives is assumed to be in the self interest of the donor state and can be conceptualized as competing foreign policy objectives.

International Explanations

The economic, security, and political interests of the donor state are best conceptualized as independent explanations that capture different aspects of the donor state's behavior in regards to foreign aid policy. Each explanation can be operationalized as a more specific empirical model that captures distinct foreign aid decision making strategies. For example, the security and economic categories, can be reduced into more specific submodels, that capture different definitions, or conceptualizations, of the donor state's security and economic interest.

This research project will reduce two models from each of Little and Clifford's three foreign policy objectives; a total of six foreign aid decision making strategies are operationalized. Each of these six models is classified as being in the interest of the donor state. A seventh model based on the interests of the recipient state, will also be operationalized.

As a foreign policy objective the national security interest of the donor state can be conceptualized as two models. The first model stresses the immediate security needs of the donor state; including mutual security agreements with recipient states, the location of United States' military bases and facilities, and the level of United States bilateral military aid. The national security explanation can also be conceptualized as the attempt to secure good relations with recipient states based on their power potential. This approach stresses military potential by considering the size of the recipient state's military, its military resources, and the size of the state's population and economy.

Each of these conceptualizations can be classified as being in the donor state's security interest. Yet, they are independent, in effect representing two different strategies for achieving the same foreign policy objective. To determine the relative influence of each it is necessary to operationalize two independent models.

The economic interests of the United States can also be promoted through two independent conceptualizations. The first approach stresses immediate economic gain by emphasizing bilateral trade relations, the level of private investment by United States citizens, and the potential for profit. These are foreign aid policies of economic self interest.

The alternative means of promoting the economic foreign policy objective is through foreign aid strategies designed to promote the economic development of the recipient state. Through the promotion of development the United States improves relations, and encourages the development of free market economic systems. As was the case with the security foreign policy objective, to test the relative influence of each approach it is necessary to operationalize two models derived from a common economic explanation.

The political foreign policy objective can be reduced to capture the political ideology and systemic stability interests of the donor state. The first foreign aid strategy is designed to promote the development of democratic institutions. The second political foreign policy objective is to promote the stability of the recipient state in an effort to protect the systemic interests of the donor state.

Each of the six foreign policy objectives outlined has been the focus considerable research and requires further consideration to justify the operationalization of the empirical models presented in Chapter Four. In this chapter each foreign aid strategy will be reviewed in detail. After reviewing the literature on the six foreign policy allocation strategies, the international explanations derived from the interest of the recipient state will be considered.

International Explanations

THE NATIONAL SECURITY STRATEGY

> "The security of the United States is related to the security and stability of nations a half a world away." (Robert McNamara, the American Society of Newspaper Editors, Montreal, Canada, 1966)

According to Deutsch, the primary foreign policy objective of any nation is to insure national survival through the promotion of its own security interests. (Deutsch:78:100-106) With the conclusion of World War Two, the United States, entered into a period of intense international competition the with Soviet Union that continues today. Foreign aid, according to the national security explanation, is a consequence of the international competition between East and West. (Liska:63:184-234)

Black, in his discussion of the strategies of foreign aid, suggested that the foreign aid policies of the United States are in part a security response to communist aggression. (Black:68:15) There is substantial support for this position in official documentation. As mentioned, under the Mutual Security Act of 1951, a collective security agreement was a necessary condition for receipt of economic aid. A.I.D. in its publication of policy objectives, as reviewed by Ohlin, adopted the level of Soviet aid allocated to the recipient state as one determinant for the distribution of United States foreign aid. This reflects a conflict oriented policy designed to prevent any recipient state from becoming overly dependent on the Soviet Union for foreign aid and developing a communist political system or a socialist economy. (Ohlin:69:19)

The security aspect of foreign aid was also acknowledged by the Clay Commission Report of 1963. The Clay Commission was formed by President Kennedy to review and make recommendations concerning the foreign aid policy of the United States. In its final report, the Commission stressed the world-wide communist threat and strongly recommended that foreign aid policy reflect the security and ideological interests of the United States. (Clay:63) Perhaps the most convincing evidence for the national security objective, however, is the Supporting Assistance Programs administered by A.I.D.. Monies appropriated under this program are allocated to reflect the immediate security interests of the United States. The program does not provide military aid per-se, rather its mission is to provide economic aid in support of United States military assistance, personnel and bases. (Black:68:17)

International Explanations

Competition between East and West produces two national security objectives that can be achieved or pursued through the allocation of economic aid. Both require acceptance of a highly competitive international system, as conceptualized by Kenneth Waltz. Waltz perceives the international system as being in a state of anarchy where nation states compete for survival. One way that this competition manifests itself is through the acquisition of allies and the socialization of the international system into spheres of influence. (Waltz:79:38-60 & 102-129)

The first security related foreign aid strategy is to use economic assistance in the acquisition and maintenance of allies among the less developed states. (Morss & Morss:82:75) Through acquisition of allies and the resulting increase in the military capabilities of the sphere of influence, the relative security of the donor state is increased. In addition, the donor state often gains access to the military facilities and potentially the military personnel of the recipient state during times of crisis.(Koplan:68:109)

In the effort to improve national security and promote the acquisition of allies, the primary consideration is the relative military capacity and militarism of the recipient state. As a consequence, those states with greater military capacity, or a high level of geopolitical power, are the most prized allies. The geopolitical power foreign aid decision making strategy predicts that foreign aid allocations will be distributed according to the relative military capacity and militarism of the recipient state. (see Figure Three)

The acquisition of allies is important to the national security of the donor state. However, allies can change sides, or fail to rally when required. The national security of any major world power, in the final analysis, requires foreign military bases. As a super power, and the core of a major sphere of influence, the United States has world wide security commitments. In order to meet these commitments, the United States requires a world wide network of military and support bases.

The second security related foreign aid strategy is to assist in the acquisition and maintenance of United States bases abroad. (Asher:70:22-27) The actual staffing of military bases is not a function of United States economic assistance as administered by A.I.D.. (Black:68:6-7) However, through the supporting assistance program A.I.D. is actively involved in providing the necessary economic assistance to support United States military bases abroad. (Legislative Reference Service:69:68-69) Also, economic assistance can be used as a means of influencing the host government by making the acceptance of United States military bases and personnel a prior condition to the allocation of monies. (Morgenthau:62:301-303)

A Foreign aid policy designed to assist in the acquisition and maintenance of foreign military bases should result in a distribution pattern caused by the location of United States bases and on the relative strength of bilateral security ties. A closely related objective of such a policy would be to limit, or disrupt, the security arrangements and bilateral relations of Eastern Block countries, by influencing the behavior of recipient states that have either close economic or military ties with the Eastern Block.

The security interest strategy predicts a distribution pattern based on the nature and strength of the recipient state's bilateral relationship with Eastern Block states. Both strategies are based on the security concerns of the United States, and they can be collapsed into a single model that measures the recipient state's bilateral relations with the United States and the Soviet Union.

International Explanations

McKinlay and Little have specified two models to capture the security interests of the donor state. The first model captures the security interest of the United States, through the operationalization of measures specified to capture the presence of United States military bases or troops and the relative strength of the bilateral relations between the recipient state and communist bloc countries. The hypothesis being tested is whether the United States allocates foreign aid based on the security interest of the United States (McKinlay and Little:79:241) (see Figure Six)

The second security model hypothesizes that the United States allocates foreign aid to the more powerful recipient states to secure desirable allies and thereby improve United States security. The second security model is operationalized as the geopolitical power model, and measures the power of the recipient state in relation to the degree of militarism, population and the size of the recipient state's economy. (McKinlay and Little:79:241) (see Figure Six)

THE ECONOMIC STRATEGY

> "Foreign economic policy is the
> use of politics to set rules
> for economic transactions

> [including foreign aid] between
> a state and/or its citizens and
> those of another state."
>
> (Pastor:80:9)

Deutsch in his book The Analysis of International Relations , (2d edition), puts forth the postulate that the economic interest of the state is a function of the state's survival and is second only to the security interest of the state. The economic interest of the state includes protection of foreign investment, preservation of favorable conditions of trade, and acquisition of title of ownership to land, resources and other categories of real economic wealth. (Deutsch:78:103) In order to secure these economic policy goals, foreign aid can be used to promote and protect United States foreign economic interests.

This theoretical justification of the economic explanation is largely consistent with Waltz's theories of international politics. To survive, according to Waltz, the nation state must adopt policies of self interest, including national security and the promotion of the nation state's economic interests beyond its borders. (Waltz:79:38-60 & 129-161) The humanitarian need and economic development of the recipient state are not significant considerations, unless they contribute to the survival of the donor state.

International Explanations

This perspective perceives foreign aid as being reflective of the economic self interest of the donor state.

Foreign aid policies can support the donor's economic self interest by expanding export markets, providing for new investment opportunities, securing low-cost sources of raw materials for import, and in general increasing the economic penetration of the recipient state. (Asher:70:27) There is substantial support for this explanation in various policy statements and proclamations.

President Kennedy, who in his inaugural address stressed the humanitarian objectives of foreign aid, also recognized that providing economic assistance gave American businessmen access to otherwise closed markets. (O±Leary:69:92) A.I.D., according to Nelson, actively promotes United States private investment as a matter of public policy. (Nelson:68:110) In addition to promoting United States economic expansion, United States foreign aid policies attempt to protect foreign investment, limit competition between United States and foreign producers, and attempts to insure that foreign aid expenditures are used to stimulate the domestic economy of the United States.

When a recipient state accepts United States foreign aid, it also accepts the under which foreign aid is extended. Many of these conditions, as mandated by enabling legislation and administered by A.I.D., are designed to protect United States economic interests. One condition, usually referred to as tied aid, requires that the goods necessary to complete an A.I.D financed project must be purchased from United States domestic suppliers and shipped to the recipient state as an import, even if the material is available in the recipient state. (Little & Clifford:65:82)

One result of this policy is that the majority of A.I.D. expenditures are used to purchase goods that are produced in the United States. Tendler notes in her book Inside Foreign AID , that in 1974 "more than eighty percent (80%) of A.I.D. funds [were] spent in the United States." (Tendler:75:73) To further promote United States economic interests and to protect United States shipping from competition, all exports from the United States for A.I.D. financed development projects must be shipped on United States commercial carriers. (Liska:63:102)

The promotion of United States investment and tied aid have tended to increase the level of United States economic penetration and activity in recipient states. A significant portion of the increased economic activity is from the United States government in the form of economic assistance, but policies of self interest also tend to increase private investment and participation as well. This has led to the expansion of United States transnational corporations in recipient states.

To protect private investments from competition, A.I.D. actively attempts to avoid financing projects which would increase competition for either United States transnational corporations or for United States domestic goods. And, finally in an effort to protect the economic interests of transnational corporations and other United States investments, policies have been adopted that prohibit the recipient state from expropriating United States property without speedy and adequate compensation. (Nelson:68:109-111)

Perhaps the best illustration that these policies are in the economic interest of the donor state, however, is the level of resentment expressed by the recipient states. The recipient states have attacked the policies of tied aid, shipping limitations, and protection of transnational corporations through the New International Economic Order (N.I.E.O.) resolutions and proposals adopted by the sixth special session of the U.N. General Assembly in 1974. (Kousoulas:85:330)

International Explanations

Section III-V of General Assembly Resolution 3202 (S-VI), which outlines specific policy objectives to implement the N.I.E.O., calls for an "international code of conduct for transnational corporations" which would in effect place transnational corporations under the exclusive regulatory control of the host or recipient state. (GA Resolution 3202(s-vi)section III-V) While United States policies limiting expropriation are not specifically mentioned, it is nevertheless clear that such policies are inconsistent with the host state's "right to nationalize or transfer ownership to its nationals" the property of transnational corporations as an expression of the "full permanent sovereignty of the [recipient] State."
(GA Resolution 3201(s-vi) section 4-e & GA Resolution 3202(s-vi)section III-V)

As with regulation of transnational corporations, the policies of tied aid and shipping on United States carriers are not specifically mentioned in the N.I.E.O. resolutions. However, full enactment would result in elimination of these policies. The N.I.E.O. calls for the exemption "whenever possible of the developing countries from all imports [from developed state to a developing state] and capital outflow controls imposed by the developed countries" and calls for increased public foreign investments (foreign aid) "in accordance with the needs and requirements" of the recipient state "as determined by the recipient countries." (GA Resolution 3202(s-vi)section II-par. d & e) In reference to shipping, the N.I.E.O. calls for more "equitable participation of developing countries in the world shipping tonnage" presumably including the shipping of A.I.D. financed developmental goods from the United States to the recipient state. (GA Resolution 3202(s-vi)section I-4 par. a)

The N.I.E.O. represents a perception of the international economic order whereby the developed states of the world benefit at the expense of the less developed states. This perception includes the concept that the economic foreign policies of the developed states, including foreign aid, are in self interest of the the developed states, and are basically exploitive to the recipient state. (McGowan & Walker:81:347-382)

References to the N.I.E.O. are being used to illustrate that the majority of the recipient states perceive the foreign aid policies of the United States and other donors as being in the economic self interest of the donor state rather than in the interest of the recipient state. Whether the economic self interest of the donor state is the paramount foreign aid strategy is a question for empirical investigation, however, there is a wide perception among several diverse sources and actors that this is the case. (see Figure Three)

There is a second foreign aid strategy derived from the economic explanation of foreign aid, that is theoretically based on the interdependence perspective of international relations, and derives some of its theoretical justifications from the modernization theory of economic development. According to the interdependence perspective, the world system is becoming smaller and increasingly economically interdependent. As a result the donor states are becoming more economically sensitive to the conditions and level of development of the recipient states. (Copper:70:159-164)

One consequence is that the economic "growth and progress of the poor countries are essential to our own [developed states] economic well being." (Sewell:80:vii) The long-range well being of all donor states, including the United States, requires a continuing and expanding world commerce, and a secure and expanding supply of raw materials. (Black:68:15-18) This requires the peaceful and sustained economic development of third world states. The developed states, including the United States, cannot indefinitely prosper in a world of poverty. (Ohlin:66:19)

International Explanations

There are subtle but important differences between a foreign aid strategy designed to promote economic development and a foreign aid strategy based on the economic self interest of the donor state. Policies of self interest are based solely on the economic needs and perspectives of the donor state, and are arguably short term policies. Such policies may hurt or retard economic development because they tend to extract capital from the recipient state. In contrast, policies that are based on the developmental needs of the recipient state, with consideration of their absorptive capacity, reflect the enlightened self interest of the donor state, and are usually perceived as long term policies.

More specifically, until the adoption of the Basic Human Needs allocation criteria in 1973, official policy included the promotion of economic development through the utilization of foreign aid monies to create the conditions necessary for the take off into self-sustained growth, as described by Rostow. (Morss & Morss:82:22-23) Rostow, in his writings on modernization theory, made several references to the important role of foreign aid and investment to promote the economic development and growth of third world states. According to this theory foreign aid, as a source of capital, was necessary to stimulate the process of economic growth. (Streeten:81:104-106) Once self-sustained growth had been achieved foreign aid would no longer be required.

The developmental foreign aid strategy also has a strong economic ideology base. Rostow theorized that the modernization process was largely a result of free market capital forces.

> "The notion of economic development occurring as the result of income shifts from those who will not spend (hoard or lend) less productivity to those who will spend (or lend) more productivity is one of the oldest and fundamental notions in economics. It is basic to the Wealth of Nations and it is applied by W. Arthur Lewis in his recent elaboration of the classic model." (Rostow:56:245)

Consequently, by promoting economic development, the United States is also encouraging the development of free market economies. Presumably, the long term foreign policy objective is to avoid becoming a free market economy in a sea of communist-socialist economies.

International Explanations

The objective of foreign aid, according to the development strategy, is twofold; the first, as stated in the A.I.D. publication "Principles of Foreign Assistance," 1963, is to help recipients "develop into self-supporting nations." (A.I.D.:63:1) The relationship between the modernization theory of economic development and a public policy of "self-supporting nations" is self-evident. But, there is a second aspect of modernization theory which is to insure that these newly developed self-supporting states have free market economies. The Congress has reinforced the second aspect of the modernization theory by "repeatedly [stressing] the need to build up private enterprise in the developing countries." (Nelson:68:51)

In order to achieve the take off into self sustained growth the recipient states must have the ability to utilize or absorb the economic assistance being extended by the donor state. Economic growth and development require certain preconditions and a policy commitment on the part of the recipient state. (Nelson:68:33-34) Consequently, the allocation of foreign aid, as conceptualized by the development strategy, is based on the economic growth potential of the recipient state rather than the economic self interest of the donor state. If a recipient state with very limited developmental potential is a major trading partner with the United States, and/or if there are substantial United States investments, the economic self interest strategy predicts a correspondingly high level of foreign aid. The development interest strategy, given the same conditions, predicts a relatively low level of economic assistance due to the limited potential of economic development.

However, the development strategy remains a derivative of the foreign policy explanation. There is unquestionably greater sensitivity concerning the requirements and conditions of the recipient states in comparison to the national security or the economic self interest decision making strategies. Nevertheless, foreign aid is being allocated for ideological purposes, and in the long term enlightened self interest of the donor state. There is no requirement or commitment to distribute aid to the poorest of the poor (whose potential for development is limited) or on the basis of the recipient state's human condition. (see Figure Three)

The economic foreign policy goal is operationalized as two models, 1) the economic self interest model and 2) the development interest and performance model. The economic self interest model is measured by trade and investment indicators and explains the distribution of foreign aid in relation to the foreign policy goal of protecting and promoting United States exports and investment opportunities. The hypothesis being tested is that the United States allocates foreign aid to reflect its own economic interest, in relation to trade and investment. (McKinlay and Little:79:240)

The second economic model measures the development potential and economic performance of the recipient state. By promoting economic growth the donor state encourages the development of free-market economies. It is hypothesized that through promotion and growth of free-market economies the donor state is acting in its own long term foreign policy interest, and those recipient states with the greatest growth potential will receive a proportionate level of foreign aid.

THE POLITICAL IDEOLOGY STRATEGY

> "The promotion of liberal democracy throughout the ±third world' provides the most enduring safeguard to Western security. Further, it can encourage a consonance of interest with low income countries." (McKinlay & Little:79:242)

International Explanations

The theoretical distinction between the security strategy and the political ideology strategy is not always clear in the literature. Many researchers collapse the two explanations into a single theoretical category. Asher, for example, considers the acquisition of bases, the prevention of imminent communist takeover, and the promotion of democracy as components of the security explanation. (Asher:71:22-27)

Other researchers including McKinlay and Little, and Koplan make a clear distinction between foreign aid allocated to reflect the security interest of the state and aid allocated for ideological purposes. (McKinlay & Little:79:242/ Koplan:68:104-107) Both strategies, however, explain the distribution of United States bilateral foreign aid within the context of the Cold War competition between East and West. As a consequence, both strategies may reflect different aspects of the same anti-communist containment foreign policy of the United States.

In order to distinguish between the two strategies, it is necessary to operationalize two independent models, one that specifies United States security interests and a second independent model that specifies ideological interests that are not related to national security. Since both strategies explain foreign aid within the context of United States self interest, both are derivatives of the foreign policy explanation.

References to Deutsch and Waltz have been utilized to justify the foreign aid strategies discussed. Both researchers specify the security and economic interests of the state as the paramount motives and causal agents behind foreign policy decisions. (Deucth:78:100-106 & Waltz :79:129-193) Both researchers base their interpretations largely on the survival motive of the nation state in the world system. The security and economic strategies considered, are reflective of the foreign policy objectives derived from the survival motives of the donor state. However, there is a second school of thought which stresses the ideology of the state, and explains the intense Cold War competition between East and West with references to the ideological incompatibility between communism and liberal democracy. (Kegley & Wittkopf:85:41)

Ideology "establishes the long range goals of a state's external behavior" which presumably can be promoted through the transfer of economic resources in the form of foreign aid. (Holsti:83:325) The foreign policy of the United States', according to this interpretation, is significantly motivated and caused by the ideological perspectives of the

United States. (Jonsson:82:91-110) For the United States, an ideologically based foreign policy includes the promotion of "liberal institutions and private enterprise" including "the development of democratic political institutions." (Holsti:83:329)

The security strategy predicts that foreign aid distribution will reflect the donor state's security interest. There is no consideration of the recipient state's regime type or its ideological base. In contrast, the political ideological foreign aid decision making strategy explains foreign aid distribution by ranking recipient states according to their ideological consistency with the United States, and predicts that foreign aid will be allocated proportionately.

The use of foreign aid to promote the development of free market economies that are ideologically consistent, from an economic perspective, with the economy of the United States has already been discussed as an important element of the development interest decision making strategy. The concern here is with the use of foreign aid to promote the development of political institutions that are consistent with the political ideology of the donor state.

International Explanations

An ideologically based foreign policy as defined by Asher, stresses the promotion and development of democratic institutions among the recipient states. The policy objective, for the donor state, is to avoid becoming a loan democracy in the wave of communist states, and to promote in its stead a world order which is ideologically compatible with the United States. (Asher:71:22-30) Koplan expresses virtually identical views, when he writes that an ideologically derived foreign aid policy is based on the proclamation of liberal values and institutions; however, the United States should not expect the development of identical institutions. Rather the United States should expect the development of liberal institutions that are uniquely developed to meet the particular needs of the recipient state. (Koplan:68:109-116)

In addition to the promotion of like institutions and a congenial world order, ideology can be used to legitimize foreign aid policies to a skeptical American public. In a liberal democracy, the foreign policy decision making process includes channels "into which existing public opinion is integrated by the officials responsible for the conduct of policy." (Rosenna:65:68) In general, the American public for the temporal period of this study has not been supportive of the United States foreign aid policy. (Hero:65:71-116) To gain additional support of unpopular policies, decision makers can utilize ideological justifications. (Kousoulas:85:99) While there is only limited backing for foreign aid policies in general, there is evidence of strong public support for ideologically based assistance. (O'Leary:67:27)

An illustration of the public's support for an ideologically based policy is the annual testimony before Congressional hearings by a variety of anti-communist interest groups. (O'Leary:67:48) However, legitimizing agents are not necessarily translated into actual policy objectives. The use of ideology by decision makers to legitimize United States foreign aid policy does not of necessity mean that there is a positive relationship between the political ideology of the recipient state and the level of foreign aid allocated to the recipient state.

One final limitation of the ideology model is that "it is unwise to assume that a country's foreign policy is shaped only by the ideological beliefs of its officials." (Kousoulas:85:99) Consequently, it is most unlikely that the ideological foreign aid decision making strategy will be the paramount explanation of United States bilateral foreign aid allocations. It is more likely that the ideological decision making strategy will be a partial explanation capable of explaining a limited portion of United States foreign aid allocations.

In particular the ideology strategy may be capable of explaining variances between two recipient states that are more or less equal in other qualities but vary in their ideological orientation. For this reason, it may be pertinent to combine the ideological model with the security and economic interest strategies to determine whether ideology has a significant additive impact on the decision making process under the conditions of ceteris paribus. (see Figure Three) However, this research question is not necessary to the primary research objective; consequently the additive effects of ideology on the allocation of bilateral foreign aid is a matter for future research.

McKinlay and Little collapse the political stability and democratic interest models into a single empirical model designed to capture both phenomena. Unfortunately there appears to be no theoretical justification for combining the two foreign aid strategies into one empirical model, nor is there support in the literature for McKinlay and Little's selection of independent variables. (McKinlay and Little:79:242) As a consequence McKinlay and Little's have misspecified the political ideology and systematic stability model, and their conclusions concerning the model are spurious.

The comparative literature concerning the measurement of democracy and stability has concluded that the two phenomena are largely independent and "that the incorporation of political stability in measures of political democracy may lead to spurious findings". (Bollen:80:384) Also, the indicators utilized by McKinlay and Little bear little resemblance to the measures and indicators developed and utilized by Bollen, Jackman, Cutright or other theorist in the field. (McKinlay and Little:79/ Bollen:80/ Jackman:74/ Cutright:67/ Bollen and Jackman:85) Finally, from the perspective of foreign aid theory, the promotion of political stability to maintain the systemic status quo may require providing assistance to recipient states that are clearly nondemocratic and show little indication of developing democratic institutions. Vietnam and Iran during the 1960's and 1970's are probably cases in point.

To avoid potential theoretical inconsistencies and spurious findings it is necessary to separate the components of McKinlay and Little's political stability and democratic interest model, and specify two independent models; one to capture the political ideology strategy and a second model to capture the systemic stability foreign aid strategy. To specify the new models it is appropriate to adopt consistent indicators presented in the comparative literature. While two models will be operationalized for this research further consideration of the systemic stability model will postponed until after review of the pertinent literature in the next section.

The political ideology model needs to measure the relative level of democratic development in the recipient state. The measurement of political democracy has been the focus of an intense debate in the comparative literature, however over the past five years (1980-1985) a consensus has developed and Bollen's model of political democracy is generally considered to be the most theoretically consistent and reliable measure currently available. Consequently it appears appropriate to adopt Bollen's model to replace McKinlay and Little's measure of democracy. (Bollen:80/ Bollen and Jackman:85)

THE SYSTEMIC STABILITY STRATEGY

> "The crux of United States interest in developing nations is the fact that they are the least stable element in the international community. Therefore, they

> are the most likely to become the scene of conflict from which the United States may be unable to abstain." (Koplan:68:106)

In order to theoretically justify the systemic stability foreign aid strategy, it is necessary to conceptualize a bipolar systemic structure and consider the United States relative position in the international system. Since World War Two the United States has been one of the two dominant world powers and has been locked in a system wide struggle for control and influence with the other dominant world power, the Soviet Union. However, within the world system the relative position of the United States, in comparison to the Soviet Union, has changed over time.

According to Waltz, the United States has had two systemic foreign policy goals; and the policy emphasis on one or the other goal is reflective of the relative position of the United States in the international system. The first systemic goal dominated United States foreign policy from the end of World War Two on into the mid and late 1960s. During this period, the United States' position in the international system was one of dominance with a substantial economic and military comparative advantage over the Soviet Union and other world actors.

International Explanations

Because the United States was the dominant world power a foreign policy designed to implement world homogeneity was adopted. (Waltz:79:194-203) However, as America's "extraordinary dominance" "diminished through a less drastically skewed distribution of national capabilities," the United States adopted systemic policies designed to maintain or stabilize the current international system. (Waltz:79:203-204)

As a tool of foreign policy, economic assistance can be utilized to achieve either systemic objective. The homogenic objective is adequately captured by the security, economic, and political ideology foreign aid strategies already presented. The distribution of foreign aid to stabilize the world system is not captured by the foreign aid decision making strategies considered. Yet, through case studies, it known that foreign aid has been utilized in an effort to stabilize regimes that are considered friendly to the United States. (Lowenthal:65:141-160)

Foreign aid can be utilized to stabilize the international system when the United States interests are "threatened [by] politically unstable regimes." (McKinlay & Little:79:242) Note that there are two necessary conditions for the distribution of economic assistance to promote stabilization of the international system.

International Explanations

First, there must be some degree of instability that presumably threatens the regime of a low income country. However, this condition while necessary is not sufficient for the allocation of United States economic assistance to stabilize the regime. The United States does not have an equal interest in maintaining each regime in the world system. Some regimes are hostile to the United States, and it is unreasonable to presume that the United States will allocate foreign aid funds to stabilize such regimes. In some cases the United States might engage in policies of destabilization in a blatant effort to replace the current hostile regime with a more friendly one. Nicaragua during the 1980s is clearly a case in point.

In order to justify the allocation of economic assistance to maintain the system, the donor state must have a foreign policy interest in stabilizing the recipient state's regime. Both conditions are necessary; the regime of the state in question must be threatened through political destabilization, and the donor state must have some degree of self interest in the maintenance of the current regime. When both conditions are met, the donor state will act to protect its interest with a transfer of economic resources in the form of foreign aid.

International Explanations

The foreign policy explanation assumes that the donor state allocates foreign aid based on the presence and degree of its self interest. Consequently, given this condition it is reasonable to presume that the donor state will act to stabilize any recipient of foreign aid in an effort to protect its foreign policy interests. However, this is not a very enlightening assumption. The only prediction that can be derived from this assumption is that destabilized recipient states will be allocated more assistance than stable recipient states. The explanatory power of the model can be enhanced significantly by including consideration of the relative level and nature of the donor state's interest. The enhanced explanatory power stems from two additional assumptions.

The first is that the donor state can be expected to react quicker and with greater generosity in direct proportion to its level of self interest. The second assumption is that the donor state will be more motivated to protecting certain types of self interest in relation to other types of self interest. For example, the United States is interested in insuring the stability of the Philippines partly because of the presence of key United States military bases. If the United States' sole interest in the Philippines was economic development, the United States would not be as concerned over political instability.

International Explanations

To incorporate the additional assumptions, it is necessary to combine the stability strategy with the other foreign aid strategies already discussed. The five foreign aid strategies considered - security, geopolitical, economic self interest, development interest, and political ideology strategies - measure the relative strength of the donor state's interest based upon competing conceptualizations of the foreign policy objectives of the United States.

By combining the models a second set of hypotheses can be generated which will enhance our understanding of the distribution of United States foreign aid. For example, the economic self interest hypothesis is that the distribution of economic assistance is proportional to the economic self interest of the donor state. By incorporating measures of systemic stability into the economic self interest model, a second hypothesis is generated: that the donor state will increase its level of assistance above the level justified by economic self interest, if said economic interests of the donor state are endangered by political instability. However, the additive effects of political instability on the other foreign aid decision making strategies is not necessary to the primary research question.

The first step is to determine whether there is a positive relationship between political stability and the allocation of foreign aid. Assuming a positive relationship, it would then be appropriate to test the additive effects of the political stability model. The systemic stability strategy will be operationalized as an independent empirical model and tested accordingly. (see Figure Eight)

The specification of an empirical model to measure political stability presents some difficulties. First, while stability has been included in the measure of political democracy by comparative researchers, particularly by Cutright, the measures specified combine or intertwine stability and democracy in a manner that makes it virtually impossible to disaggregate the measurement of stability from the measurement of political democracy. (Cutright and Wiley:69) For example, Cutright develops a scale to measure the level of democracy in the Legislative and Executive branches of government, that "penalize each nation for political instability". (Cutright:63:256) Unfortunately when the democratic element of the measure is removed the scale and measure become meaningless. (Cutright:63:256-58)

The second difficulty is that political instability is an abstract concept, and in "the case of high level abstractions (such as ±economic development' or ±political instability') the design involves concepts that possess multiple characteristics, any one of which may be inadequate in capturing or defining the complex nature of the phenomenon in question." (Geller:82:36) Consequently, the measure of political stability needs to be comprehensive including several indicators to capture the complexity of the stability phenomenon. Geller, in his analysis of the causal relationship between economic modernization and political stability, developed a model to measure political instability which produced reliable results. To replace McKinlay and Little's measures, Geller's model of stability will be adopted. (Geller:82)

EXPLANATIONS BASED ON THE INTERESTS OF THE RECIPIENT STATE

> "According to the recipient need model... the amount of aid allocated to a [recipient] state is in proportion to its need, and the distribution of aid will reflect the relative needs of recipient states." (McKinlay and Little:79:237)

Foreign aid can be allocated to reflect the foreign policy interests of the donor state, or to reflect the interests of the recipient state. Explanations based on the interests of the recipient state reject the foreign policy explanation; replacing the foreign policy objectives of the donor state with altruistic motives. Rather than acting from a sense of self interest the donor state motives are humanitarian, and reflect the basic human needs of the recipient states.

For example, White considers the basic human needs approach as being "associated with an explicit morality; a prescriptive view of individual and collective responsibility". (White:76:12) The altruism of the recipient interest explanation is justified as the "right" or "decent" thing to do and is reflective of what the United States stands for in the world. (Asher:70:35-37) The source of this morality "stems from the ideals and actions of the American people" that have been "nurtured and developed by the religious, political and personal freedoms" that are part of the American heritage, ideology and political institutions. (Black:68:20)

The presumption of the recipient interest explanation is that recipient states are ranked according to their humanitarian or basic human needs. Those states with the greatest need receive a proportionate level of foreign aid. The recipient interest explanation is unique in that the criteria for determining the allocation of foreign aid monies is nonpolitical and based on the needs of the recipient state. (Mogenthau:62:301-302) As a consequence, the recipient interest explanation has the potential to falsify the foreign policy explanation. To do so, however, the recipient interest explanation must explain a substantial portion of the distribution of foreign aid.

In the consideration of the recipient interest explanation a clear distinction must be made between the form, or type of aid being allocated by the donor state, and the context, or the reasons and motives, which cause the donor state to allocate foreign aid to a specific recipient state. Foreign aid funds administered by A.I.D. are classified, for budgetary purposes, by four primary categories; Food and Nutrition, Education and Human Resource Development, Selected Development Problems and Population Planning. (Starting in 1979 the Food and Nutrition category was reclassified as Agriculture, Rural Development and Nutrition, and the Population and Health category was separated effectively creating two categories see A.I.D. Country Program Summary and Budget Request) Each of these budgetary categories can be conceptualized as providing humanitarian relief or as addressing basic human needs.

International Explanations

However, the humanitarian form of the aid being provided does not necessarily mean that the distribution of aid is determined by the humanitarian need of the recipient state. Foreign aid in the form of humanitarian relief, such as rural development or food allocation, "can perform a political function when it operates within a political context." (Morgenthal:62:301) Foreign aid allocated within a political context, regardless of its form, is reflective of the foreign policy of the donor state, and can be explained by one of the six foreign aid strategies derived from the foreign policy explanation, considered in the previous sections.

The recipient interest explanation is not a reference to the form of bilateral foreign aid administered by A.I.D.; rather it is a consideration of the context of foreign aid, and attempts to explain the allocation of foreign aid based on the basic human needs of the recipient state. An example which illustrates the distinction between the form of aid and the context of its distribution is the case of the Dominican Republic in the early 1960's.

Lowenthal conducted an extensive case study of the events that accrued in the Dominican Republic after the assassination of Rafael Trujillo in 1961. Lowenthal's analysis concentrates on the United States response and policy actions that followed Trujillo's assassination, including the use of foreign aid funds to influence the external and internal policies of the Dominican Republic.

The form of the economic assistance utilized to influence the policies of the Dominican Republic included monies designated for projects designed to address basic human needs such as nutrition and rural development. Whatever the form, Lowenthal concluded that these funds were being allocated for the purpose of achieving fairly specific foreign policy objectives. (Lowenthal:65)

Consequently, regardless of its humanitarian form, aid was being allocated within a political context with the intent, on the part of the donor state, to influence the political behavior of the recipient state. Because the events that followed Trujillo's assassination clearly illustrate the distinction between form and context the case bears greater consideration.

After the Trujillo assassination the primary United States foreign policy objective was to prevent Rafael's brothers from seizing power and continuing the dictatorship of the Trujillo family. To achieve this goal the United States used the threat of force. The threat was successful and Rafael's brothers withdrew. However, the threat of force could not effectively influence the formation of a new government that was both anti-Castro (external policy objective) and pro-democratic (internal policy objective). To achieve these foreign policy goals the United States turned to a "more subtle instrument" of foreign policy to create "a viable interim regime pledged to conduct free elections." (Lowenthal:65:145) The "more subtle instrument" was foreign aid.

Foreign aid was first employed as an inducement to influence the formation of the Council of State, an interim government acceptable to the United States. The cancellation of foreign aid was then employed as a threat to prevent a successful military coup from retaining power. The United States also used foreign aid to insure that the Council of State held new national elections, and finally to support the elected government that replaced the interim government in December 1962. (Lowenthal:65)

The case of the Dominican Republic demonstrates the use of humanitarian aid within a political context. The recipient interest explanation is a question of context and distribution rather than a question of the type or form of assistance. For foreign aid to be allocated in the interest of the recipient state there must be no intent, on the part of the donor state, to affect a political outcome.

The primary foreign aid policy classified as being in the interest of the recipient state is the humanitarian, or basic human needs policy. However, there are two additional foreign aid policies that might be classified as being in the interest of the recipient state. The first is the developmental interest decision making strategy. If one assumes that economic development is in the best interest of the recipients of foreign aid, then the strategy can be classified as a recipient interest policy. In support of this classification it can be argued that economic development is probably the only long term policy capable of improving the basic human condition of low income states.

However, as noted in the consideration of the development interest strategy, the donor state is interested in promoting a specific type of economic development. If the recipient state is interested in developing an economy based on the economic principles of scientific socialism, the United States will probably not provide the necessary developmental foreign aid. It is because of this economic ideological element that the development strategy has been classified as being a derivative of the foreign policy explanation. Still, providing that the recipient state is independently interested in developing a free-market economy, the development strategy might be classified as being in the interest of both the recipient and donor states.

The second foreign aid policy that might be classified as being in the interest of the recipient state is the basic human rights policy. To classify a basic human rights policy as a recipient interest policy it is necessary to assume that protecting human rights is in the long term interest of all states and peoples. However, it could be argued that the definition of human rights is depended on political ideology and culture. This issue is more complex than it first appears.

Certain concepts of human rights, such as freedom from torture, are basically universal. Other concepts, such as freedom of religion, and assembly are more culturally and ideologically dependent. Whether a basic human rights policy should be classified as being in the interest of the recipient state or in the ideological interest of the donor state depends on the definition of human rights, and on the intent of the donor state. If the definition of human rights is based on the United States Bill of Rights, and the intent is to foster American values, the policy is properly classified under the political ideology decision making strategy.

From a methodological perspective, operationalization of a model to capture a basic human rights strategy presents some difficulties. Basically it is simply very difficult to develop an accurate measure of basic human rights. In addition the basic human rights policy, as adopted by the United States Congress during the early to mid 1970s, includes a number of limitations and conditions designed to limit aid to governments that violate basic human rights without hurting the poor citizens of the same state.

In some respects the basic human needs policy is in conflict with a basic human rights policy. How does one punish governments and still provide aid to the poorest of the poor? There is no intent to operationalize a model to capture a basic human rights policy. For the reasons given, only the humanitarian, or basic human needs, strategy will be operationalized as an empirical model and tested for significance. Given Lowenthal's case study and the empirical evidence it appears unlikely that the recipient interests explanation will not falsify the foreign policy explanation. However, some level of explanatory power for a basic human needs foreign aid policy should be expected, given public policy statements, amendments to the 1961

Foreign Assistance Act, and the level of support for humanitarian aid expressed by the public. This is particularly true for the decade of the 70's.

THE HUMANITARIAN STRATEGY

> "Sometimes dismissed as soft-headed and illrelevent it remains durable and patent, it involves justice and decency and the moral basis for leadership among nations."
>
> (Asher:70:33)

Through the 1950's and 60's United States foreign aid policy was dominated by the Pearson Report which stressed Rostow's doctrine of the stages of economic growth, and later by the report of the Clay Commission which stressed the security needs of the United States. By the 1970's, however, a change in policy perspective occurred. There was a general acknowledgment of the limits and failures of Rostow's theories concerning the take-off into self-sustained growth. (Streeten:81:109) This, combined with increasing Congressional disapproval of the Vietnam War, caused a substantial shift in the official goals and objectives of United States bilateral foreign aid policies. (Congressional action will be considered in Chapter Three).

Of particular import is the 1973 Amendment to Chapter I Section 102 of the Foreign Assistance Act of 1961. Which stated quite clearly that humanitarianism was to become the primary policy objective of United States bilateral foreign economic aid.

> "United States bilateral development assistance should give the highest priority to undertakings submitted by the host government which directly improve the lives of the poorest of their people and their capacity to participate in the development of their own countries." (1973 Amendment to the 1961 Foreign Assistance Act)

The policy objective of the 1973 basic human needs amendment was to shift the allocation of United States bilateral foreign aid to reflect the basic human needs of the recipient states. Those states with the greatest need were to receive a larger proportion of foreign aid. The adoption of the 1973 basic human needs amendment was the result of conflict between the Executive and Congress. The amendment would probably not have been adopted except for Congressional dissatisfaction over the Vietnam war. (see Chapter Three)

The impact of the 1973 basic human needs amendment is a question for empirical investigation, however there is evidence that the United States has "made visible attempts to initiate and carry out a basic needs strategy by adding specialized staff members and designing special projects". (Hoadey:81:154) The 1973 amendment was followed in 1975 by policy statements that created distribution criteria designed to implement the 1973 basic human needs amendment. (Hoadey:81:151-152)

In addition the United States formally recognized the special needs of the fourth world states, (the poorest of the poor) in reference to their basic human needs and increased foreign aid requirements in the pre-conference documents for the UNCTAD Paris conference on the Least Developed States in 1981. More specifically the United States during the conference accepted the position of the Group B Block (Developed Western Donor States) that increased aid was critically needed to improve the human condition in the Least Developed Countries. (UNCTAD Documents A/CONF. 104/PC 19 Add .5 and Add .7)

Whether this apparent shift in policy is reflective of an actual shift in aid distribution is questionable. There are indications that the difficulties of distributing aid to the poorest of the poor has prevented full implementation of the 1973 basic human needs amendment. (Hoadey:81:155) And, if one reads the 1973 amendment with the eye of a lawyer, it call for a shift in aid to "improve the lives of the poorest" of the recipient state's population. Within each recipient state there are people whose basic human needs go unfulfilled daily. The 1973 basic human needs amendment calls for aid to be distributed to the poorest segment of the population and does not necessarily preclude the distribution of bilateral foreign aid to reflect foreign policy concerns.

The 1973 amendment maybe more of a question of intrastate distribution rather than a question of shifting aid allocation to the poorest of the recipient states. And finally, if the basic human needs criteria is operating within a political context it will reflect the foreign policy interest of the donor state, even if the aid is being distributed to the poorest of the poor within the recipient state.

International Explanations

McKinlay and Little operationalize a model to test the recipient need explanation. But, as was the case with the democratic stability model, there is are specification problems with their Recipient Need Model. Mosley in his review of McKinlay and Little's research questioned both the specification of the Recipient Needs model and the estimation procedure utilized to measure the explanatory power of the model. (Mosley:81:245) McKinlay and Little, based on the use of ordinary least squares statistical techniques, concluded that there was "no support for the hypothesis derived from the recipient need model" (McKinlay and Little:79:243)

Mosley challenges the use of ordinary least squares noting that "this estimation procedure produces biased estimates if the independent variables in question are endogenous, ie in addition to influencing the level of aid flows are also influenced by them in a process of simultaneous causation". (Mosley:81:246)

For their Recipient Need Model, McKinlay and Little operationalize measures of percapita GDP, growth rate of percapita GDP, and domestic capital formation as a percentage of GDP, as independent variables. However, GDP as a measure of economic activity, influences the flow of foreign aid and is simultaneously influenced by the flow of foreign aid; resulting in simultaneous causation which violates one of the necessary conditions of the ordinary least square statistical technique.

Mosley, to produce unbiased results, adopts two stage least squares, where the level of aid is the dependent variable in the first stage and percapita GNP is the dependent variable for the second stage. Mosley's concern for simultaneous causation is justified, but there is a simpler correction technique that does not require the adoption of two stage least squares.

The potential violation of the causal relationship stems from the foreign aid component of the GDP or GNP measure. To avoid simultaneous causation the GNP measure can be modified by subtracting the foreign aid component from the measure. (adjusted GNP = GNP - AID) In this manner the endogenous component of the independent variable is removed avoiding both simultaneous causation and the adoption of two stage least squares statistical techniques.

In addition to questioning McKinlay and Little's estimation procedure Mosley also questions their specification of the recipient need model. Mosley notes that McKinlay and Little's model fails to measure the recipient state's economic dependence which, according the Mosley, has an impact on the recipient state's need for foreign aid. Mosley also rejects the growth of GDP percapita measure, noting that "if this variable were accepted as a valid indicator of need, then amongst the countries in world most needful...would appear Switzerland...and Kuwait". (Mosley:81:246-247)

Mosely respecifies the recipient need model using "five indicators of recipient need, namely percapita GNP, literacy rate, life expectancy, country size and the balance of payments". (Mosley:81:247) Using two stage least squares Mosley tested the validity of his recipient need model against several different donor states for the years 1963, 1971 and 1977. The results of Mosley's analysis are mixed. However, in general the saliency of the recipient need model increases as one moves from the 1960's through the 1970's. (Mosley:81:249-253)

Unfortunately Mosley does not report regression coefficients for individual donor countries; consequently the relative saliency of the independent variables for the United States cannot be determined from Mosley's research. Mosley does report that the proportion of United States aid allocated to the poorest of the poor, or the recipient states with the lowest percapita income (less than $300), increased from 52.8% in 1971 to 69.6% in 1977, an increase of 16.8% over six years. The increase in the allocation of aid to the poorest of the poor is consistent with the predictions of the humanitarian foreign aid decision making strategy; especially in reference to the potential impact of the 1973 basic human needs amendment to the Foreign Assistance Act of 1961.

Mosley's recipient need model attempts to capture the level of "poverty of the recipient country in terms of both national income and in terms of self sufficiency". (Mosley uses the term ±self sufficiency' in relation to the ability of the recipient state to provide for the basic human needs of its citizens)(Mosley:81:248) However, in relation to self sufficiency Mosley clearly under specifies his model.

There are six phenomena that are related to the basic human need, or self sufficiency, of third world states: health, education, food, water supply, sanitation, and housing. (Hicks and Streeten:79:578) To measure these phenomena the most often used indicators include: life expectancy, literacy, calorie intake per capita, and infant mortality. Unfortunately there is no adequate indicator for housing. (Hicks and Streeten:79:578-579) Mosley operationalizes only two of these indicators, life expectancy and literacy.

International Explanations

To measure the level of poverty in relation to national income Mosley adopts percapita GNP, country size and balance of payments. Mosley's, national income measures are the most salient, and the preponderance of the explanatory power of his Recipient Need Model stems from these three independent variables. (Mosley:81:248-253) However, until calorie intake percapita and infant mortality rate are included in the model, the relative explanatory power of Mosley's recipient need model cannot be determined with confidence. Consequently, the recipient need model operationalized in Chapter Five will include; Mosley's measures of national poverty and the basic human needs measures suggested by Hicks and Streeten.

CONCLUSION

As noted in the introduction there are two approaches to explaining the allocation of bilateral foreign aid. One approach focuses on international causes, while the second approach stress the domestic politics of the donor state. The intent of this chapter was to review the research literature that complies the international approach. The domestic literature will be reviewed in Chapter Three.

The propositions found in the international research literature suggest that the allocation of bilateral foreign aid across recipient states can be classified as being in either the interest of the donor state or the recipient state. Because both classifications are derivatives of the international approach they share a number of theoretical parameters.

Each adopts the nation state as the unit of analysis, and specifies the donor state as the decision making unit of interest. The donor state is assumed to be a rational choice decision maker. Consequently, both the the donor interest and recipient need models apply the rational choice paradigm to explain the allocation of bilateral foreign aid. As a rational actor the donor state ranks recipient states according to their relative utility, and allocates foreign aid proportionally. The distinguishing factor between the recipient need and the donor interest models is not the the nature of the decision making process; but in the criteria used to rank alternatives.

The donor interest model hypothesizes that the donor state ranks foreign aid alternatives based on the foreign policy objectives of the donor state. In contrast the recipient need model hypothesizes that the donor state ranks foreign aid alternatives based on the needs of the recipient state. And further, it is assumed that the donor state allocates foreign aid without the anticipation, or intent, of national gain.

The donor interest model can be reduced to capture six distinct conceptualizations of the foreign policy interest of the donor state; economic self interest, developmental interest, security interest, geopolitical power interest, political ideology interest and systemic stability interest. Each submodel is distinct in the criteria utilized to rank foreign aid alternatives, and the submodels can be categorized as independent foreign aid decision making strategies. Unlike the donor interest model, only one decision making strategy can be reduced from the recipient need model, the humanitarian, or basic human needs strategy.

While it is possible to derive seven decision making strategies from the international explanation, it seams unlikely that the donor state bases its foreign aid allocation decisions solely on one ranking criteria. It seams more likely that the donor state assigns a weight to each decision making strategy, and bases its decision on some composite measure of relative utility. According to this hypothesized scheme the final allocation of bilateral aid is based on a ranking of alternatives that includes the consideration of the relative, or weighted, utility of each foreign aid decision making strategy; in effect creating a composite measure of utility for each recipient state. The recipient state ranked first, by the composite measure of utility, will receive a proportionate level of foreign aid.

For example, there is empirical evidence to suggest that the security decision making strategy has the greatest utility to the donor state. Consequently, the utility of the security interest policy will be greater than the utility of the other strategies. As a result recipient states with significant donor state security interests will tend to be ranked higher than states without significant security interests. However, the combined weighted utility of a second state with significant ideological consistency, strong economic ties, and great humanitarian need may be ranked higher than the first state; providing the ranking criteria is based on a composite measure of utility.

Whether one foreign aid decision making strategy dominates the allocation of United States bilateral foreign aid, or whether the donor state bases its decision on some composite measure is a question for empirical investigation. The empirical literature considered suggest that the security interest of the donor state dominates the allocation of bilateral foreign aid. However, other foreign aid decision making strategies were also found to be significant. If the donor state does base its funding decisions on relative utility it should be possible to determine the weight of each decision making strategy by operationalization of theoretically consistent models and testing their explanatory power.

All scientific inquiry can be conceived as an extension of previous research and the experimental design and proposed models herein are no exception. The review of the empirical research raises four questions which require further investigation.

The first is whether there is adequate support for the humanitarian explanation to justify continued testing of the model; and, providing there is adequate theoretical support, which indicators should be operationalized to capture the phenomenon in question? Second, while the empirical literature strongly supports the foreign policy explanation there remains the question of the relative saliency of the foreign policy models operationalized, and the transitive order of foreign policy goals. A closely related question is the correct specification of the political ideology and systemic stability models.

Third, does the empirical evidence justify the independent consideration of military and economic assistance? And fourth, is there empirical evidence to suggest that domestic events effect the allocation of foreign aid? These questions will be addressed from the international approach, however, some of the issues being raised here also effect domestic modeling and require further consideration in the next Chapter.

The empirical support for the humanitarian decision making strategy derived from the recipient interest explanation is mixed and inconclusive. Using Peace Corps data Cohn and Wood tested for the impact of the basic human needs criteria adopted by the United States on Peace Corps programming, and the allocation of Peace Corps Volunteers. Their conclusions are mixed. While noting a strong organizational commitment to the implementation of a basic human needs approach, Cohn and Wood conclude that the "data strongly suggest that Peace Corps programs in the more developed countries reflect basic human needs goals ...more closely than programs in the less developed countries". (Cohn and Wood:80:228) Indicating that the basic human needs criteria has effected intrastate allocations of material and manpower; but has not caused a shift in resources to the poorest of the poor recipient states.

In addition to Peace Corps programs being more effective, from a basic human needs perspective, in middle income countries Cohn and Wood found that only 15.9% of all volunteers work in recipient states with percapita incomes of $200 or less, while almost half work in middle income countries. (Cohn and Wood:8:318) There conclusions are inconsistent with the allocation of resources to the poorest of the poor as predicted by the humanitarian explanation.

However, as Cohn and Wood point out their results are based on indirect measures, and are not conclusive. Part of the allocation of resources is due to the difficulties of implementation. Peace Corps Volunteers are usually attached to host country agencies, consequently the capabilities and the absorptive capacity of the host country may prevent full implementation of a basic human needs approach. (Cohn and Wood:80:328-329) And, some recipient states resist Peace Corps programs because they wish to avoid increased numbers of United States citizens.

Hoadley, in a more comprehensive consideration of the impact of basic human needs criteria, reaches an almost identical conclusion. Hoadley concluded that the donor states sincerely adopted the basic human needs criteria. However, due to host state limitations and related difficulties of implementation, the basic human needs approach has not resulted in significant long term changes in foreign aid programming or in the allocation of resources. (Hoadley:81)

However, Mosley reports a significant increase in the allocation of United States bilateral aid to recipient states with less than $300 percapita income, which supports the predicted allocation pattern. And, while Mosley's recipient need model is underspecified, he concludes that the model cannot be falsified, and predicted that as "one moves from the 1960s in time ...the explanatory power of the recipient need model increases". (Mosley:81:253) The only researchers to reach a definitive conclusion concerning the humanitarian explanation are McKinlay and Little, who misspecify their model and base their rejection of the humanitarian explanation on inappropriate estimation procedures. (McKinlay and Little:77:79)

The answer to the question posed, concerning the humanitarian decision making strategy, is that based on a review of the empirical literature the model cannot be adequately supported or falsified. Consequently, further inquiry is appropriate. In regards to the specification of indicators, it appears that the adoption of McKinlay and Little's measures of national poverty, combined with the basic human needs indicators suggested by Hichks and Streeten, will be theoretically consistent and comprehensive. (see Figure Seven)

International Explanations

Based on the findings of Kato and McKinlay and Little, one must conclude that foreign aid is a tool of foreign policy. This does not, however, of necessity falsify the humanitarian explanation. It should be noted that neither McKinlay and Little or Kato consider the allocation of foreign aid during the 1970's. As a consequence there is no measurement or consideration of the impact of the 1973 basic human needs amendment. In addition some question remains concerning the transitive order of the foreign policy goals over time. Any comparison between Kato's and McKinlay and Little's research results is limited because of the variance in model specificaion, indicators and temporal period. Nevertheless, the relative saliency reported varies significantly. (see Figures Five and Table One) Of particular interest is Kato's findings concerning the low explanatory power of the cold war model and the high salience of the economic need, or development interest model. (see Figure Five)

Additional inquiry to determine the transitive relationship between foreign policy goals is justified. Considering that McKinlay and Little's models are more complex, in that they consider a total of twenty-five indicators compared to Kato's ten, it seems appropriate to replicate McKinlay and Little's research where theoretically consistent. As noted, however, the recipient need model will be respecified. Also the the Political Stability and Democratic Interests model will be replaced with Bollen's model of political democracy and Geller's model of political stability, respectively. (see Figure Seven) As a matter of expediency, those indicators that McKinlay and Little did not find significant will be dropped from the analysis.

In reference to the third question posed, whether the empirical evidence justifies the independent consideration of military and economic assistance, our conclusions must rest on Kato's research. As illustrated in Figure Five the relative saliency of Kato's indicators varied significantly between economic and military aid. In addition, from a theoretical perspective there appears to be no rational to support a causal relationship between the humanitarian decision making strategy and military foreign aid. Consequently, to compare the foreign Policy and recipient interest explanations it is appropriate to limit one's consideration to economic aid.

The final question is whether there is empirical evidence to suggest that domestic events influence foreign aid allocations. The evidence is weak, but there is support for a hypothesized relationship between foreign aid allocation decisions and domestic events. First, both Kato and McKinlay and Little reported significant findings for more than one model. All of McKinlay and Little's Donor Interest models were significant for at least 30% of the temporal period, and Kato reported significant findings for three of his five models. (see Figures Five and Table One)

These findings could be the result of a single decision maker trying to achieve several foreign policy goals simultaneously, or the result of a compromise between domestic decision makers with competing rank order priorities. Second, Kato concluded that the explanatory power of his domestic economy model was significant; more significant than the cold war model. (Kato:69:201-202) This indicates that domestic economic events may influence foreign aid decisions, and therefore effect the allocation of bilateral aid.

The final evidence in support of domestic influence on the allocation of foreign aid is the most intriguing. McKinlay and Little report the regression coefficients for each donor interest model by year. (McKinlay and Little :79:249-250) If one reviews their findings carefully there is a clear pattern where by the development interest model is more significant during election years and is less significant between elections. In 66% of the cases reported the development interest model is significant during election years. The level of significance drops to 20% for years with no elections. A similar relationship is found with the economic self interest model which is significant 50% of the time during election years and only 20% of the time during between election years. (McKinlay and Little :79:249-250) It appears that the allocation of foreign aid is effected by domestic elections. (see Table Two)

Each of these cases could be the result of a statistical aberration or caused by phenomenon other than domestic events. The question is not whether they prove that domestic events influence the allocation of foreign aid, they do not. However, they do justify further inquire into the potential effects of domestic events on the allocation of foreign aid.

FIGURE THREE

INTERNATIONAL FOREIGN AID DECISION-MAKING STRATEGIES FOUND IN THE LITERATURE

DECISION MAKING STRATEGIES	PREDICTED FOREIGN AID ALLOCATION PATTERN
DONOR INTEREST;	
security interest	to states with strong mutual security ties and/or with US military bases
geopolitical power	to states with substantial military capabilities or other measures of significant power capabilities
economic self-interest	to states with significant trade and financial relations with the US
developmental interest	to states with the greatest potential for economic development
political ideology	to states that are ideologically consistent with the US through the development of democratic institutions
systemic stability	to states that are politically unstable and where it is in the US's systemic interest to prevent instability
RECIPIENT INTEREST	
humanitarian	to states with the greatest basic human need

FIGURE FOUR

KATO'S EXPLANATORY MODELS AND INDEPENDENT VARIABLES

MODELS	INDEPENDENT VARIABLES
Strategic interest model	the presence or absence of communist backed subversion proximity to communist border military alliance with US
Cold war model	amount of trade with Soviet Union the political support given to US foreign policy stands in the U.N. the presence or absence of communist bloc aid to the county
Trade model	a county's contribution to U.S. trade
Economic development model	the level of GNP per-capita
Domestic economy model	the level of deficit in balance of payments of U.S. the proportion of aid program in GNP of the U.S.

FIGURE FIVE

COMPARISON OF MILITARY AND ECONOMIC AID IN TERMS OF SALIENCE OF B'S

MODEL	HIGH SALIENCE	MEDIUM SALIENCE	LOW SALIENCE
Military Assistance	alliance geography threat	trade economic communist trade domestic economy	balance of payments Soviet trade U.N. voting
Economic Assistance	geography trade balance of payments	economic need communist aid domestic economy U.N. voting	threat Soviet trade alliance

Military R Squared =.4904 Economic R squared =.1206

(Kato:69:207)

FIGURE SIX

MCKINLAY AND LITTLE'S EXPLANATORY MODELS AND INDEPENDENT VARIABLES

MODELS	INDEPENDENT VARIABLES
Recipient ** Need Model	per-capita aid per-capita GDP per-capita calory consumption number of doctors per hundred population size of international liquidity holdings as a percentage of imports rate of growth of real GDP gross domestic fixed capital formation as a percentage of GDP
US Overseas Economic Interest	US trade domination US gross trading ties investment income investment balance
Geopolitical Interest Model	population gross domestic product (GDP) gross international liquidity holdings military resources militarism
Security Interest Model	US security ties communist bloc trade domination communist bloc trading ties communist bloc security ties domestic communist support
Development Interest Model	per-capita GDP rate of growth of constant per-capita GNP gross domestic fixed capital formation size of manufacturing sector size of the mining sector international liquidity holdings
Political Stability & Democratic Interest Models **	party bans central assembly bans number of main executive changes number of military coups period under military rule

** Models to be respecified, see figures #7 & #9
(McKinlay and Little:79:239-242)

FIGURE SEVEN

RESPECIFIED RECIPIENT NEED MODEL

SOURCE	INDEPENDENT VARIABLES
Mosley:81	adjusted per-capita GNP balance of payments populations as an indicator of recipient state's absorptive capacity
Hicks & Streeten:79	life expectancy literacy rate calorie intake infant mortality (per 1000 births)

FIGURE EIGHT

RESPECIFIED POLITICAL IDEOLOGY AND SYSTEMIC STABILITY MODELS

POLITICAL IDEOLOGY

SOURCE	INDEPENDENT VARIABLES
Bollen 1980	political rights civil liberties

SYSTEMIC STABILITY

SOURCE	INDEPENDENT VARIABLES
Geller 1982	number of strikes number of riots number of anti-gov. demonstrations number of assassinations incidents of guerrilla warfare number of governmental crises

TABLE ONE

THE ANNUAL SALIENCE OF MCKINLAY AND LITTLE'S EXPLANATORY MODELS AS MEASURED BY STANDARDIZED PARTIAL REGRESSION COEFFICIENTS BY ELECTION AND NON-ELECTION YEAR

½ YEAR MODEL½	60	61	62	63	64	65	66	67	68	69	70
development interest*			S		S				S	S	S
economic interest**	S		S			S					S
security interest	S	S	S	S	S	S	S	S	S	S	S
political power	S	S	S	S	S	S	S	S	S	S	S
political instability& & democracy			S	S	S	S	S	S	S		S

Recipient Need Model is not significant.
S = Significant relationship for year
* Development interest Model:
non-election year significance = 20%
election year significance = 66%
** Economic Interest Model:
non-election year significance = 20%
election year significance = 50%
(Mckinlay and Little:79:249)

CHAPTER THREE

DOMESTIC INSTITUTIONS AND FOREIGN AID

> "Since all [of the foreign aid policy] goals can rarely be accomplished simultaneously, policy-makers are forced to weigh the relative value of each goal and rank them in a hierarchy of priorities."(Pastor:80:254)

The international approach to explaining foreign aid decisions perceives the donor state as a unitary decision maker providing assistance either in pursuit in its own self interest, or for altruistic purposes. In contrast, the domestic approach conceptualizes United States bilateral foreign aid decisions as being the result of compromises between competing interests, and policy objectives.

The need to compromise is the result of the disposition of power across domestic institutions which in effect gives certain domestic institutions veto power over the allocation of foreign aid monies. The decision making processes of the domestic institutions vary in their policy goals, legal authority and decision making environment. These differences create a competitive and dynamic decision making process which prevents the donor state from acting as a unitary actor and from pursuing a consistent set of policy objectives.

The differences between the international and domestic approaches are primarily the result of differences in theoretical perspectives. The international approach is derived largely from the realist perspective. McKinlay and Little explicitly draw a relationship between their findings and the realist perspective concluding "that the importance attached to power and security interests is consistent with the image of the international system advanced by the realist school." (McKinlay and Little:79:247)

Kato implicitly accepts the basic premises of the realist perspectives by his failure to operationalize the humanitarian explanation. Kato's only variance from the realist perspective lies in the operationalization of a domestic economic model. And one of Kato's indicators, the level of deficit in balance of payment, is more a measurement of the donor state's economic self interest then a measure of domestic economic influences. (Kato:69:202)(See Figure Four) In contrast, the domestic approach relies upon the theoretical perspectives of public administration; maintaining that foreign aid decisions are the result of organizational dynamics and budgetary theory.

US Domestic Explanations

There are important similarities between the two approaches. Both are concerned with the same phenomenon, and both structure their analysis within the theoretical parameters of the rational paradigm. They differ primarily in their specification of the decision making unit, and in the set of prioritized policy goals and preferred decision alternatives. Chapter Four will address these issues in some detail and propose an analytical scheme that permits the operationalization of theoretically consistent models to test the decision making strategies derived from the international approach, at the domestic level.

Before operationalizing theoretically consistent models at the sub-national level of analysis, it is necessary to describe the specific foreign aid decisions being considered and to determine the legal authority and environmental characteristics of the domestic institutions that influence the allocation of foreign aid funds. In order to achieve this goal, it is necessary to consider the nature of foreign aid decisions, the disposition of constitutional authority across domestic institutions, and finally to consider the decision making process within the Executive and the Legislative Branches respectfully.

Several analytical schemes suggested by domestic researchers will be considered, but of particular importance are Anthony Downs' classification of bureaucratic power, Richard Fenno's scheme of Congressional decision making, and Ripley and Franklin's model of Executive and Congressional relations in the formation of United States foreign policy.

THE NATURE OF FOREIGN AID DECISIONS

> "The level of United States aid is determined not by any rational criteria, such as the international targets, but by a series of compromises between the positions of the Administration and the many different voices of Congress." (Cunningham:74:92)

The theoretical parameters of the rational choice paradigm require the clear identification and specification of the decision making phenomenon of interest. The observable allocation of foreign aid monies across recipient states is the result of four decisions which, while not necessarily independent, are nevertheless distinct phenomena. The first decision is on the part of the recipient state which must decide whether to accept bilateral foreign aid and if so, by which donor. This issue will be considered in Chapter Four, and will not be readdressed here, except to note that the decision making unit being examined in this research is the donor state and its domestic institutions. Consequently, the decisions of the recipient state are not a consideration.

The allocation of foreign aid funds require three substantive decisions on the part of the donor state; 1) whether a given state qualifies for aid; 2) whether to provide military or economic aid, or both; and 3) how much, or the level of aid to provide. United States qualification criteria for bilateral aid is complex, somewhat arbitrary, occasionally contradictory, and changes almost annually. The complexity in United States foreign aid qualifications is primarily the result of almost annual Congressional amendments to the Foreign Assistance Act of 1961. (Liska: 63:102/Tendler:75) But, the Executive is also partly responsible: when "there has been a change between Democrat and Republican Presidents, the new administration had felt almost an obligation to make changes" in bilateral foreign aid policy. (Cunningham:74:68)

Several researchers have noted or commented on the complexity and inconsistencies of formal foreign aid criteria, often citing Congressional amendments to the Foreign Assistance Act of 1981 as examples of legislative influence and independence. But, other than noting its complexities, both descriptive and empirical researchers have tended to avoid a comprehensive analysis of qualification criteria. The primary exceptions are the studies that test the relationship between the basic human needs and human rights allocation criteria adopted in 1973 through 1975. These studies are limited, however, in that they do not consider the entire population of potential recipient states. The research parameters are limited to the consideration of states currently receiving United States bilateral aid. (Schoultz:81/Colon and Wood:80/ Hoadley:81/ Streetan:77)

Some of the qualification criteria have been noted elsewhere, and there is no intent to provide a substantive consideration of the topic. However, as a research question, the decision as to whether a specific state qualifies for United States bilateral foreign aid is largely unexplored and the literature is underdeveloped. The underdeveloped nature of the research on the impact of United States statutory foreign aid criteria raises interesting research questions and opportunities. The research question is highly complex.

For example, Cunningham reported that in 1969 there were a total of "sixty-eight qualifications to be met for a development loan." (Cunningham:74:96) To investigate the effects of statutory qualification criteria on the allocation of United States bilateral foreign aid requires the operationalization of theoretically consistent models capable of capturing a significant portion of the statutory criteria. These models once specified would be regressed against both recipient and non-recipient states. Since the research question is one of qualification, rather than the level of assistance, it would probably be appropriate to operationalize the dependent variable, the level of bilateral aid, as a dummy variable.

Hopefully, in this manner, the set of aid receiving states would contain a number of substantive characteristics that were distinct from the characteristics of the non-recipient states. Based on positive outcomes, generalizations could then be developed concerning the relative salience of statutory qualifications for receiving United States foreign aid.

However, there is no intent to pursue this question further and one can only speculate on the theoretical and methodological complexities that would result from the specification of empirical models to capture statutory criteria. The research question of concern to this analysis, as outlined in the introduction, is whether there is significant differences in the foreign aid decision making determinants across domestic institutions. The qualification question is intriguing, but not necessary to the primary research question, and therefore will not be considered further except where pertinent.

The second decision required of the donor state, prior to the allocate foreign aid funds, is whether to distribute military or economic aid. To find the estimator for the dependent variable, aid per capita, McKinlay and Little divided population into the total aid combining both military and economic aid. (McKinlay and Little:77:65-67) (McKinlay and Little, in their 1977 research, also adjust the dependent variable for the size of the recipient states economy, a more complete consideration is provided in the Research Notes) By combining the two forms of aid, McKinlay and Little may have biased their findings. Of particular concern is the inclusion of military aid to test the validity of the humanitarian model.

There is theoretical support, as previously noted, for a relationship between economic development and military aid. However, there is no rationale to suggest that military aid is distributed on the basis of the humanitarian need of the recipient state. The inclusion of military aid is irrelevant to the humanitarian foreign aid strategy, and its inclusion may have biased the regression coefficient downward, potentially suppressing a significant relationship between economic aid and the humanitarian foreign aid policy objectives.

The obvious and primary objective of military aid is the security of the donor state. Consequently it is reasonable to assume a high correlation between the security interests of the United States and the distribution of military aid. The question is whether the strength of the relationship is adequate to suppress any significant differences between the distribution of economic foreign aid and the distribution of military foreign aid in McKinlay's and Little's findings.

Kato's findings, however, illustrate the potential difference in distribution patterns between the two forms of assistance. Of equal interest are the findings of Gist and his consideration of mandatory expenditures in the defense sector. Using multiple regression analysis, Gist tested military and economic assistance to determine the level of non-incremental budgetary change over time. (Gist:74:12-15) Gist, based on the outcome of his empirical analysis, concluded that: "economic assistance is disadvantaged in the budgetary process relative to military assistance. The coefficient suggests that on the average the Administration asks for more military assistance every year, while asking for less economic assistance. The Congress in turn, has chosen to appropriate a larger share of the military assistance request than for economic assistance." (Gist:74:24)

Of equal importance, it is unclear whether the combined estimator is theoretically consistent with the rational choice paradigm at the sub-national level. To apply the rational choice paradigm to an organization, there must be some minimum level of consistency in organizational structure and in the decision making process. There are important differences in the military and economic decision making process.

Within the Executive branch, different agencies dominate the two forms of foreign aid and,as noted by Mason "military assistance and economic development assistance compete to a certain extent for foreign aid funds." (Mason:64:20) It is also interesting to note that the most comprehensive proposed reform of A.I.D. (by President Nixon in 1970) specifically called for the formal legal separation of the two forms of aid.

Yet, by combining the two forms of aid into one estimator to capture the dependent variable, McKinlay and Little have implicitly assumed that the decision making process and organizational structure that is responsible for the distribution of military aid is fundamentally the same as the process utilized for economic foreign aid decisions. Whether these concerns are justified at the nation state level of analysis is a matter of conjecture. However, when the unit of analysis is reduced to the sub-national level, the consequence of any differences in the structure and decision making process between the Executive and Legislative Branches takes on added importance.

Whether there is any significant difference in the distribution of military and economic aid can be tested by independently regressing the foreign aid models against the two categories of aid. However, this is a matter for future research and is beyond the parameters of the current research project. But to avoid any potential theoretical inconsistencies, only economic foreign aid, administered by A.I.D., will be considered and included in the dependent variable.

There are five main forms of economic aid; development loans, technical assistance, supporting assistance, a contingency fund, and contributions to United Nations agencies and other multilateral aid institutions. (Cunningham:74:81) With the exception of multilateral aid (contributions to United Nations and other international agencies), A.I.D. is the primary United States agency responsible for the administration of United States economic foreign aid.

The predominance of A.I.D. activity is involved in the distribution and administration of development loans and project grants. Of the four forms of aid administered by A.I.D. only supporting assistance relates primarily to military criteria. (Black:68:18) Since the parameters of this research project do not include military aid or economic aid designed to support military facilities or assistance, the supporting assistance program administered by A.I.D. will be removed from the dependent variable.

In addition, emergency aid or disaster relief will not be included in the analysis. Almost by definition, these forms of aid are distributed based on natural events rather than through some rational decision making process designed to achieve specific policy objectives, whether they be national, institutional, individual, or international. However, it should be noted that this definition of the dependent variable implicitly creates a best case research design for the recipient needs model. It is reasonable to assume that if the United States distributes any foreign aid based on the needs of the recipient state, other than disaster assistance, it will be the development loans and grants administered by A.I.D..

The third and final decision on the part of the donor state is how much aid to allocate to a specific recipient state. Why the donor state decides to allocate a specific level of assistance to a given recipient state has been the primary focus of foreign aid research, including this research project. The review of the international literature on foreign aid illustrates the complexities of attempting to rationally explain the process of deciding how much aid to allocate to a specific recipient state. At the international level, the funding decision is basically a "good policy" decision in that the donor state must determine what constitutes good international policy in relation to the allocation of foreign aid. When the funding decision is reduced to the sub-national level of analysis the complexities are increased, as the differences between institutions and the implications of the budgetary process are added to the analysis of foreign aid decision making.

The complexities of this process are best illustrated by reviewing the constitutional disposition of power across domestic institutions that effect the foreign aid decision making process, followed by a consideration of the decision making process within the Executive and Legislative Branches.

THE DISPOSITION OF POWER AND FOREIGN AID DECISIONS

> Most foreign policy decisions "cannot be implemented without prior Congressional authorization, and funding legislation subsequently signed into law by the president."
>
> (Whale:83:11)

In the development of United States international policy, or foreign affairs, the President is usually considered the dominant actor. The dominant role of the President in foreign relations is partly the result of constitutional prerogative, but is also the result of historic development. Constitutionally, the President, as commander-in-chief, is responsible for national security and has the authority to negotiate treaties, to recognize governments, to make diplomatic and administrative appointments, and to enter into Executive agreements. (Crabb & Holt:84:11-18/ U.S. Constitution Article II Section 2) The ability to enter into Executive agreements has been of particular importance in the post World War II era in that "such agreements have accounted for almost eighty-five percent (85%) of the understandings reached between the United States and foreign countries." (Crabb & Holt:84:15-16)

In addition to constitutional prerogatives, and perhaps of more import, over the "two hundred years of American history the tendency has been toward Executive preeminence in nearly every aspect of the foreign policy process." (Crabb & Holt:84:11) The general trend of the last two hundred years does not necessarily indicate that during each period or that each President has dominated foreign relations decision making. The Constitution provides for the disposition of powers across the Executive and Legislative Branches; consequently, the relative preeminence of the President in foreign relations has fluctuated considerably over time, and during the temporal period of this study.

The Senate, in particular, is given "a unique [constitutional] role in the foreign policy process, advice and consent to treaties and the confirmation of executive appointments." (Crabb & Holt:84:42) These constitutional prerogatives have traditionally made the Senate the primary focus of Congressional action in the area of foreign relations policy. (Fenno:73:151) However, the House is not without influence in the area of international policy particularly in regards to the allocation of funds. By tradition all appropriation measures start in the House and, in relation to foreign aid policy, the ability to control the purse includes significant influence over the allocation of foreign aid funds. (Crabb & Holt:84:47/ Whale:82:81) Traditionally, the House has played a subordinate role to the Senate in international policy, but with the advent of annual multibillion dollar foreign aid authorizations and appropriations, the House has tended to become more active and has sought to reverse its traditional role. (Crabb & Holt:84:44)

Because of the disposition of power between the Executive and Legislative Branches, most international policies "cannot be implemented without prior Congressional authorization and funding legislation subsequently signed into law by the President." (Whale:82:11) Consequently, the locus of decision making authority has shifted overtime, usually favoring the Executive but shifting to Congress for specific temporal periods.

Woodrow Wilson, for example, writing as a graduate student in 1884, raised the issue of the role of the Executive and the Congress in foreign relations, and concluded that Congress was the dominant branch. (Whale:82:11) As President, Wilson's conclusions were proven at least partly valid when the Senate rejected the Versailles Treaty and membership in the League of Nations. Presidents Harding and Hoover during the 1920s and the 1930s, reached similar conclusions and commented that the Congress was superior in foreign affairs. (Whale:82:11)

However, the relative power of Congress is at least partly dependent upon the leadership role and personality of the President. Harding and Hoover were both passive Presidents and may have permitted the Congress to dominate as a matter of choice. Wilson, by his active leadership role in personally representing the United States at the Versailles Treaty negotiations, may have alienated the Republican Senate and caused the Senate rejection.

In contrast, President Roosevelt was able to persuade Congress to defer to Presidential leadership, including the allocation of some Congressional constitutional prerogatives. For example, the Reciprocal Trade Agreement Act of 1934 for the first time allocated control of tariff rates and conditions, traditionally a Congressional constitutional prerogative, to the Executive Branch. The passage of the 1934 Act began a period of unparalleled Presidential leadership in foreign relations that was to last nearly forty-five years. (Whale:82:12) It was during this period of Presidential dominance and initiative that foreign aid was adopted as formal United States policy under the Truman Administration and A.I.D. was established under the Kennedy Administration.

Except for the immediate post war period when President Truman was able to form an alliance with the Chairman of the Senate Foreign Relations Committee, Senator Vandenberg, to insure the passage of the Greek-Turkish Aid Program (1947) and the Marshall Plan (1948), foreign aid has not been popular with the Congress. (Crabb & Holt:84:40-48) There are two primary causes for the unpopular nature of foreign aid policies in the Congress. The first is that foreign aid has been generally unpopular with the American public.

The second is the lack of domestic beneficiaries. Because of these two characteristics Congress has generally considered support for foreign aid a potential political liability. (Crabb & Holt:84:25) One consequence of the lack of popularity for foreign aid policies in Congress has been continued Congressional criticism of AI.D.. The President, in contrast, has continued to support the foreign aid program and has been willing to invest significant Presidential prestige to insure the annual passage of foreign aid authorizations and appropriations. (Tendler:75:39)

US Domestic Explanations

The continued and strong Presidential support for a the foreign aid program is an indication that the Executive Branch has found foreign aid a useful instrument of international policy. Presidents have routinely used foreign aid to buy the allegiance of less developed states, extend the security interests of the United States, and have usually considered foreign aid a necessary instrument in the Post WWII competition between East and West in the international system. (Morss & Morss:82:75-76)

As a instrument of international policy, foreign aid can accomplish specific goals which cannot be achieved through diplomacy or force alone. The use of aid by the Kennedy Administration to influence the events of the Dominican Republic in the early 1960s has already been noted. In addition, the fall of the Diem regime in Vietnam has been tied to the unwillingness of the United States, under the leadership of President Kennedy, to provide additional economic or military assistance as long as Diem remained in power. (Mason:64:41)

The Kennedy Administration also relied on economic assistance to induce Latin American Sates to join the Alliance For Progress. (Mason:64:70-74) The utilization of foreign aid as a means of advancing United States international interests continued under the Johnson, Nixon and Carter Administrations. President Johnson used both economic and military assistance to help finance the Vietnam War, and by the late 1960s a substantial portion of United States foreign aid, to the displeasure of Congress, was allocated to Vietnam. (Cunningham:74:75) President Nixon was unable to utilize foreign aid to help finance the Vietnam War because of Congressional resistance, however, the promise of significant levels of economic aid was used by the Nixon Administration to help persuade North Vietnam to end the war. (Crabb & Holt:84:230)

In general, when President Carter took office in 1977, it was anticipated that foreign aid would be utilized to help initiate several major changes in North South relations. (Sewell:80:14-15) In particular, President Carter attempted to utilize foreign aid to help implement his Human Rights policy. (Schoultz:81:149-151) However, these initiatives on the part of President Carter generally did not have significant substantive impact on foreign aid policies.

The use of foreign aid as an instrument of international policy has led to regular and persistent changes in foreign aid policy when there is a change in the administration. The impact on foreign aid policy when the party of the presidency changes has already been noted. (Cunningham:

74:68) But, the impact of personal Presidential leadership is not limited to changes in the President's political party. Tendler, in her study of A.I.D., noted that one of the environmental inconsistencies faced by the agency was the varying degree of support from the Executive, and presumably the President. (Tendler:75:24)

The relationship between A.I.D. and its Presidential sovereign is critical to the agency's continued survival. However, there appears to be more support for the policies of foreign aid than for the agency itself. Within two years of the passage of the Foreign Assistance Act of 1961, President Kennedy appointed the Clay Commission to recommend changes in United States foreign aid policy and administration. (Pastor:80:272-273) President Johnson preoccupied with the Vietnam War, made no recommendations for substantive changes in A.I.D..

President Nixon, however, commissioned another committee to review the entire development assistance policies of the United States. The committee, which assumed the name of its Chairman Randolph Peterson, made recommendations that would have effectively disbanded A.I.D. and allocated its function to other executive departments including the formal separation of military and economic foreign aid programs. (Pastor:80:277-278) The bill died in committee during the 1970-71 session which also marked an important turning point in Congressional Executive relations concerning foreign aid.

In its relations with its Presidential sovereign, A.I.D. is in a precarious situation. The continued existence of the agency and its programs is partially reliant on an Executive coalition led by the President. However, A.I.D. is not necessary to the continuation of foreign aid policies, and can probably expect continued Presidential support only as long as its willing to support the policies, priorities and desires of the President.

THE FOREIGN AID DECISION MAKING PROCESS IN THE EXECUTIVE BRANCH

> "The Marshall Plan, the Mutual Security Act, the Foreign Assistance Act and the Alliance for Progress-all have been created by the Executive, and with a concerted public relations campaign, they have been sold intact to the Congress."(Pastor:80:284)

Economic foreign aid, in the form of development loans, technical assistance, and the contingency fund, are project oriented in that the monies appropriated are limited to the financing of specific developmental projects. A significant portion of A.I.D. foreign assistance decisions are concerned with the evaluation of specific project proposals and the review of on going projects. (Tendler:75:56-58,93-99) The process of developing a project proposal and its accompanying request for funds begins each year in the Washington office of A.I.D.. The Washington office sends to A.I.D. missions in the field detailed instructions for proposed projects in the upcoming fiscal year. The instructions also include a detailed analysis of the previous year's activities including evaluations of outstanding authorizations. (Nelson:68:55-56)

Through this process the Washington office of A.I.D. actively influences the development of project proposals. However, A.I.D. is a highly decentralized agency and the actual drafting and cost estimation of development projects is completed by the A.I.D. mission located in the recipient state. (Tendler:75:12-13, 25-26, 36) Each major recipient state has an A.I.D. mission which is highly independent and consists of a director and the necessary support staff. (recipient states without missions are assigned to missions of nearby states for administrative purposes) (Cunningham:74:73-74, 94-96)

US Domestic Explanations

Annually, each mission submits to the Washington office a detailed evaluation of the recipient state's economy, reports on the progress of each project within its jurisdiction, and proposes new projects based on the annual instructions from the Washington office. For each project there is an "Activity Data Sheet" which outlines the purpose, or developmental goal of the project and provides a brief analysis of the project's history; including A.I.D. expenditures, and the financial participation on the part of the host state and other donors.

Based on these documents and related information on the host state, the Washington office evaluates each project proposal and develops the agency's annual budgetary request. (Nelson:68:56) However, A.I.D. is not an independent decision maker. At each step in the project proposal and evaluation process, there is participation by other executive agencies.

A.I.D. staff at the mission level are attached to the United States Embassy in the recipient state. The Ambassador must approve each project proposal prior to its submission to the Washington office of A.I.D.. The review at the mission level usually includes the local military assistance group and personnel from United States agencies with responsibilities for the administration of foreign assistance, such as the Peace Corps. (Nelson:68:56-57) One consequence of the inter agency activity at the mission level, is that the annual evaluation of the recipient state's economy, the report on A.I.D.'s activities, and proposals for new projects are the result of a joint decision making process. However, the local A.I.D. mission is the primary participant the "[amount of aid] allocated to that country depends primarily on the case putout by the country mission." (Cunningham:74:95)

The inter agency decision making process continues and is intensified during the review of mission reports and funding proposals by the Washington office. A.I.D. is a "semi-autonomous agency within the State Department." (Cunningham:74:69) The Secretary of State has the legal authority to review all A.I.D. decisions; however, the A.I.D. administrator, who is appointed by the President, generally operates with a high degree of independence. (Cunningham:74:73) This level of independence should not be construed to indicate that A.I.D. decisions are independent or that the Department of State and other federal agencies do not fully participate in each major funding decision.

It is more reasonable to assume that A.I.D. has accepted or adjusted its decision making process so that direct participation by the Secretary of State is unnecessary. Of particular interest are the conclusions of Tendler who reports that A.I.D. has displaced its substantive policy goals with "the goals that belong to outside entities with interest counter to the agency's." (Tendler:75:50)

It is usually assumed that the principal goal of any organization is its own survival and maintenance, and the replacement of substantive agency goals with symbolic goals is an indication that the agency is operating in a hostile environment. Symbolic goals are adopted as a means of increasing external support in order to insure continued survival. (Gordon:82:244-246) This appears to be the case with A.I.D.. (Tendler:75:50) This point can be further illustrated by considering the relative power setting of A.I.D. within the Executive Branch.

According to Downs, the relative power setting of bureaus is dependent on the bureau's relationship with key actors who control or effect the bureau's external environment. The most important actors in the external environment include the sovereign, rivals, beneficiaries and sufferers, suppliers, and allies. (Downs:67:44-47) In regards to each of these categories, A.I.D. appears to be at a disadvantage. Consequently, A.I.D. operates within a hostile environment and has limited power capabilities. Each of these characteristics of the outside environment will be considered in some detail. However, please note that the relationship between A.I.D. and its Presidential and Congressional sovereign has already been considered in relation to the constitutional disposition of power.

During the review of mission proposals in Washington, the process of interagency decision making continues and the influence of outside agencies is intensified. A.I.D. is the primary agency for the allocation of United States bilateral aid, but it is not the sole agency. About one half of the total of United States economic foreign aid falls outside A.I.D.'s jurisdiction. (Cunningham:76:71) In addition, a number of none aid agencies, that are actively involved with international policy, attempt to influence A.I.D. allocations to reflect their independent substantive policy goals. As a consequence, A.I.D. has a number of agency rivals within the Executive Branch.

A.I.D.'s rivals in the determination of foreign aid policy include the Departments of State, Treasury, Agriculture, Commerce, the Export-Import Bank, the Bureau of the Budget (or OMB), and the Peace Corps. With the exception of the Peace Corps, each of these rival agencies has some substantive authority, or institutionalized participation, in the formation of A.I.D.'s budget, and in the distribution of economic foreign aid.

The participation of the Peace Corps is limited to the statutory mandate that every effort be made to cooperate and coordinate the activities of the two agencies. (Cunningham :74:74) And, while the Department of State has substantive legal authority over the Agency for International Development, it does not appear as if the Department of State extensively interferes with A.I.D.'s decisions. However, one must presume that if there is a conflict between the diplomatic goals of the Department of State and the foreign aid allocation decisions of A.I.D. that the priorities of the Department of State would take precedence.

Of more import is the institutionalized joint decision making process between the Department of Agriculture and the Export-Import Bank. (Eximbank) Under the statutory requirements of the Agricultural Trade Development and Assistance Act of 1945 (P.L. 480, or the Food for Peace Program), and the Foreign Assistance Act of 1961 as amended, the Department of Agriculture and A.I.D. share administrative responsibility for the Food for Peace Program; "as a general rule the Department of Agriculture is responsible for procuring food supplies while A.I.D. is responsible for deciding who is to receive" food aid. (Cunningham:74:70) The dual administration of the Food for Peace Program has given the Department of Agriculture an important role in the actual distribution of food aid and in "assessing the overall need for food aid." (Cunningham:74:70)

The lending criteria of the Export-Import Bank is wholly commercial, and therefore is not technically a form of development assistance, because the flow of economic resources is not at a concessional rate. (Cunningham:74:70) However, through the Export-Import Bank's membership and participation in the Development Loan Committee, whose members also include the Assistant Secretary of State responsible for Economic Affairs and a representative of the Treasury Department responsible for Economic Finance, the Export-Import Bank is able to influence A.I.D. development loan policy. "This insures that A.I.D. does not accept any loan request without Eximbank, being given the opportunity to see if its services would meet the need." (Cunningham:74:70)

The policy objective is to limit A.I.D. development loan activity to those projects that do not qualify for funds on a commercial or near commercial basis. However, there is no requirement for the Export-Import Bank to finance a loan that has been refused by the Development Loan Committee. As a consequence, the Export-Import Bank has the authority to claim jurisdiction and effectively veto an

A.I.D. development loan, while simultaneously refusing to participate or provide funding from its own resources.

The Development Loan Committee also provides a limited opportunity for the Treasury Department to participate in the allocation of United States bilateral foreign aid. Treasury's primary form of participation however, stems from the Department's responsibilities concerning the international balance of payment. (Tendler:75:48) To control the balance of payments between the United States and recipient states, the Treasury has used its authority to influence the general flow of bilateral economic aid to the point that the Treasury has acquired a virtual veto power over specific projects administrated by A.I.D. because of balance of payment concerns. (Tendler:75:44-45)

In a similar manner, the Commerce Department has gained significant influence, if not veto power, over A.I.D. funding decisions in regards to the promotion of United States exports. The influence of the Department of Commerce extends beyond the requirements of tied aid, which were discussed in Chapter Two, to include the concept of additionality which maintains that United States bilateral aid should increase United States exports beyond the level that would have occurred through normal commercial channels. The additionality concept has caused A.I.D. to select capital projects "with the potential for follow up orders," in an effort to increase United States exports. (Tendler:75:46)

The relative influence of the Departments of Treasury and Commerce in their efforts to pursue their own international policy requirements are significant to the point that Tendler concluded that the substantive policy goals of A.I.D. have been replaced by the balance of payments and export promotion goals of the two cabinet departments. (Tendler:75:48) A.I.D.'s rivals for the control of United States bilateral foreign aid policy have been largely successful in that their goals apparently dominate A.I.D. project review and funding decisions. The relative success of A.I.D.'s rivals is due in part to the nature of A.I.D. programs and beneficiaries. A.I.D.'s programs and substantive policy goals have never been well understood and the complexities of economic development are not easily transformed or equated with specific problem solving tasks or programs. (Tendler:75:25)

The ambiguities of A.I.D.'s formal policy goals make it easy to displace these goals with the more tangible policy objectives of promoting a positive balance of payments with recipient states, and the goal of promoting United States exports. In addition, the maintenance of a positive balance of payments directly benefits United States domestic financial markets and banking interests, and export promotion directly benefits United States manufacturers, exporters, and shipping interest. In contrast, it is widely recognized that the beneficiaries of A.I.D. programs are not American citizens or voters. (Morss & Morss:82:83) All of which weakens A.I.D.'s power setting in relation to its foreign aid policy rivals.

Downs defines sufferers as those who are adversely affected by the agency's operations. (Downs:67:46) Considering A.I.D.'s operations, it is difficult to identify a domestic group which is adversely affected by foreign aid. However, it must be remembered that each decision to fund a specific development project is also a budgetary decision. If one considers the budgetary process as a zero sum situation where budgetary allocations to one agency of necessity require a trade off in dollar allocations to competing agencies and programs, then A.I.D.'s budgetary allocations are in direct competition for funds with domestic programs that have strong constituencies. (Gist:74:861-862)

Applying competitive budgeting theory or zero sum schemes to help explain the power settings of A.I.D. requires further theoretical development. However, in relation to the perspective of individual Congressmen or Senators faced with a decision to fund a domestic program which benefits voters or funding a program which benefits foreign recipients, competitive budgeting theory has relevance.

The basic premise of competitive budgeting theory is that agencies attempt to build political support for their programs to "withstand continuous attacks upon a program's resource base by competing claims." (Natcher & Bupp:73:963) The lack of domestic beneficiaries weakens A.I.D.'s competitive capabilities. As a consequence, even though A.I.D. operations do not directly cause domestic suffering, its lack of beneficiaries weakens the agency's ability to protect its resource base from the continuous attack of other agencies with strong domestic support.

A.I.D. is aware of the weakness of its budgetary position and is quick to point out that the majority of its expenditures are used to purchase goods and services from American suppliers. And, in an effort to protect its resource base, and increase its influence and support in Congress, A.I.D. publishes and distributes to members of Congress a comprehensive list of foreign aid domestic expenditures by State and Congressional district. (Morss & Morss:82:81)

US Domestic Explanations

The extent to which the suppliers of foreign aid goods and services constitute an influential interest group is an open question with contradictory conclusions across researchers. Mason, writing in 1964, concludes that there are strong domestic interests that benefit from foreign aid and support the program. (Mason:64:17) Liska writing during the same period makes similar observations and concludes that there are "economic interests within the United States which try to shape the foreign aid program so as to help themselves." (Liska:63:28) And, finally in 1967, O'Leary noted that the National Chamber of Commerce plays an important role during foreign aid hearings and that occasionally interests groups form alliances with Congress and A.I.D.; forming temporary subgovernments to mobilize support for specific aid policies. (O'Leary:67:54-58)

In contrast, Tendler speaking on the subject directly, concludes that there is no significant domestic constituency, and that domestic suppliers are surprisingly inactive in their support of A.I.D. operations. (Tendler:75:39) A second potential source of support is the general public, however, no source reviewed by this researcher has identified significant public support for United States foreign aid programs, and when asked the open ended question, "Do you think there is anything for which the government should be spending less money than it is at present?" the most frequent response was foreign aid. (Morss & Morss:82:83/Hero:65:79)

These highly divergent conclusions reported by foreign aid researchers appear to be partly the result of time. There appears to have been more support from suppliers and other allies during the early 1960s, and over time the level of active political support has apparently dissipated. However, some portion of this difference in opinion concerning the level of political support maybe the result of the differences between the Food for Peace program and other forms of economic aid. There is a clear distinction between the level of support for the Food for Peace Program and other forms of economic aid. Mason noted and commented on the strong support for Public Law 480 (Food for Peace) expenditures among farmers "who want to disburse of agricultural surpluses." (Mason:64:26)

More importantly, Ripley and Franklin in their consideration of foreign aid policies as reported in Congress, the Bureaucracy and Public Policy , classified the Food for Peace Program as being structural foreign policy. (See Figure Nine) Structural foreign policy has many of the same characteristics as domestic distributive policy; including a strong subgovernment structure that provides political support, and has an active role in public policy decisions. (Ripley & Franklin:84:100-101, 218-219) The members of the subgovernment include the Department of Agriculture's Foreign Agricultural Service, the domestic farm interest groups and lobbies, and most members of the agricultural authorization committees in both houses of Congress. (Ripley & Franklin:84:219)

The direct benefits reaped by the suppliers of agricultural surplus have formed a strong political alliance in support of the Food for Peace Program. In contrast decisions concerning other forms of economic aid are strategic foreign policy decisions, which are made primarily in the Executive Branch and are substantially influenced by the President without significant subgovernment support or influence. (Ripley & Franklin: 84:100-101, 228-229) (see Figure Nine)

The potential impact of the agricultural lobby, on the allocation of economic assistance, can be tested by operationalizing P.L. 480 funds, as a dependent variable, and regression the measure against the foreign aid decision making models. Of particular interest would be any relationship between United States domestic farm prices and the allocation of aid. In addition, by comparing the allocation of P.L. 480 funds with the allocation of A.I.D. administered economic assistance, it may be possible to determine whether the decision making units utilize the two programs to achieve different policy objectives.

For example, if the recipient needs model is the most successful model in explaining the allocation of P.L. 480 funds, it would indicate that the decision making units allocate food aid on the bases of need, while other forms of assistance, both economic and military, might be allocated to maximize the utility of competing policy strategies.

It is inappropriate to presume that economic assistance is without interest group support all together. The evidence clearly indicates that the public is generally indifferent and the suppliers of foreign aid goods and services, for whatever reason, do not actively support the foreign aid program except for Public Law 480. Nevertheless, each year the number of interest groups testifying before Congress in support of the foreign aid program far outnumber the interest groups opposed. Of particular importance are the humanitarian interest groups. (O'Leary:67:48-50, 112)

The influences of these groups maybe more significant than first appearances suggest. They are committed to their cause, and the combination of moral justification and altruistic motives has a strong appeal which has been noted by researchers, such as Black. However, the potential impact of these groups remain limited in that it is unlikely that these groups have adequate support to influence the reelection of individual Senators or Congressmen. They probably have an effect on the level of foreign aid expenditures and qualification criteria but, in general, except for the Food for Peace Program, A.I.D. has few allies in its efforts to secure a budgetary base.

Anthony Downs' system of determining the power setting of bureaus contains five elements which are pertinent to this research. The characteristics of A.I.D. have been reviewed in relation to four of these elements; rivals, beneficiaries and sufferers, suppliers, and allies. The remaining element, the sovereign, has been considered in relation to the constitutional disposition of power, but a more thorough consideration is necessary. However, it is appropriate to first review the power setting of A.I.D. in relation to the four elements considered, and to draw some preliminary conclusions.

In relation to its rivals, A.I.D. is at a comparative disadvantage. The Departments of Treasury, Commerce, and Agriculture are all older than A.I.D., have more permanent and larger staffs, and have well established constituencies and relations with Congress, including strong subgovernments. The position of the Department of State and the Export-Import Bank is probably not quite as strong as A.I.D.'s other rivals, but in comparison to A.I.D., it appears clear that both have greater political power resulting in a comparative advantage. Only the Peace Corps does not appear to be more politically powerful than A.I.D..

This situation is aggravated by A.I.D.'s lack of domestic beneficiaries, particularly when one considers the relative domestic benefits and constituencies of A.I.D.'s rival bureaus. The beneficiaries of A.I.D.'s rival bureaus increase the pressure on A.I.D. and make the agency's power setting even less tenable. The lack of domestic sufferers, no doubt, helps A.I.D.. At least there are no victims bitterly complaining before Congress as is the case with certain regulatory agencies.

However, if one extends the concept of sufferers to include competitive budgeting theory, all other agencies can be classified as suffering some loss of financial support because of monies spent on foreign aid. This point is of limited importance, except that it illustrates the difficulties A.I.D. faces before Congress. Even during periods of budgetary expansion, few agencies receive their total budgetary request, and when a Congressman needs to cut elsewhere to increase expenditures for a favored program, A.I.D. provides a convenient target.

Support from agricultural suppliers appears to be A.I.D.'s primary domestic ally. It is questionable whether this support benefits A.I.D. or is directed at the Agriculture Department. It is interesting to note that Ripley and Franklin did not include A.I.D. in the Food for Peace subgovernment. Consequently, the support from these interest groups might conceivably hurt A.I.D. by increasing the relative power of a rival agency. There is some support from other suppliers, such as shipping, the home building industry, manufacturers and exporters desiring access to markets, and consulting firms who do business with A.I.D.. (O'Leary:67:58/ Mason:64:26)

But, in general the only consistent ally of A.I.D. appears to those interest groups who support a humanitarian policy. These interest groups are not acting out of self interest, but from altruistic motives. Their influence is difficult to determine, but one should not underestimate the influence of an altruistic, and moralist perspective. Many of these same groups are also suppliers of private aid and have been successful in motivating significant numbers of people to donate and assist in the distribution of millions of dollars of private foreign aid annually.

However, one is forced to conclude that A.I.D. has limited support from its suppliers or allies.

The only supportable conclusion, in review of the domestic foreign aid literature, is that A.I.D.'s political power is limited and its organizational environment is hostile. One consequence of this hostile environment is constant and continual criticism from other Executive agencies and Congress. Tendler has concluded that criticism of A.I.D. has become institutionalized. (Tendler:75:48-50)

As a result of A.I.D.'s weak power setting, its rival agencies have been successful in dominating the agency in effect substituting their own interests and policy goals for the substantive goals of A.I.D.. Another consequence is that A.I.D. is "unusually dependent on a substantial investment of the Executive power and prestige." (Tendler:75:39) United States economic aid policy is basically a creation of the White House, and the formation of A.I.D. as the paramount administrating agency for United States economic assistance is a creation of President Kennedy. While the level of support for A.I.D. and economic assistance has varied from President to President, it nevertheless appears clear that A.I.D. and economic assistance is dependent primarily upon the relationship between A.I.D. and its Presidential sovereign.

US Domestic Explanations

Anthony Downs defines the sovereign as "any organization or person who has legal authority over the bureau." (Downs:67:44) Given the weak power setting of A.I.D. and the preponderance of influence exercised by its foreign aid policy rivals, A.I.D.'s sovereigns could conceivably include the Departments of State, Treasury, Commerce and Agriculture. However, it seems more reasonable to limit consideration to the domestic institutions with constitutional authority over funding decisions; the Executive and Congress. The Executive Branch led by the President is usually considered to be the main focus of foreign relations decision making and policy formation. (Crabb & Holt:84:7) The question is whether A.I.D.'s second sovereign, the Congress, is an active or passive participant in the foreign aid decision making process.

CONGRESS AND FOREIGN AID POLICY

> "On the substance of [foreign aid] policy, it is fair to say both that the executive tends to prevail when there is conflict and that, through the compromises necessary to reduce or resolve conflict, congressional impact on the ±big picture' of policy is also sizable, even if not finally controlling."(Ripley & Franklin:84:229)

US Domestic Explanations

From the adoption of foreign aid as formal policy at the end of World War II through the late 1960s, the President clearly dominated the formation of foreign relations policy in general and foreign aid policy in particular. One reason for the dominant role of the President was the willingness of Congress to defer to the President, a trend started by President Roosevelt in 1934. This trend affected all areas of international policy including foreign aid. (Crabb & Holt:84:7) Congress, while critical of foreign aid and never willing to appropriate one hundred percent (100%) of the funds requested, was nevertheless been willing to defer to the Executive Branch and cooperated by enacting the requested enabling legislation and approving administrative reorganizations. (See Figure Two)

A second reason for the willingness of the Congress to defer to the President was the lack of adequate information concerning foreign aid policies. (Fenno:73:30) It was assumed that the President had access to information that was unequaled. Consequently, it was assumed that the intent and structure of the proposed foreign aid budget represented informed and sound international policy. (Crabb & Holt :84:19) By the end of the 1960s both conditions began to change and the Presidential coalition faced an active and concerned Congress.

US Domestic Explanations

The end of forty-five years of Congressional deference to the President was caused by the war in Vietnam. As the war became less popular and casualties mounted, Congress, particularly the Senate, became more active in its willingness to challenge the President in foreign relations. As the willingness to challenge the President increased, so did the capacity of Congress to formulate independent policy initiatives based on its own staff and sources of information.

Between 1955 and 1974, Congressional staff increased by three hundred percent (300%). In addition, there were important changes in the legislative support system which increased the capacity of Congress to evaluate policy and develop independent policy initiatives. (Pastor:80:18-21) This increase in decision making capacity combined with a willingness to challenge Presidential leadership had an important impact on United States foreign aid policy.

Congress has always been active in its consideration of foreign aid policy. The tendency of Congress to establish additional eligibility criteria by amending the Foreign Assistance Act of 1961, has already been noted. These amendments in effect "are a means of asserting legislative content in the field of foreign aid." (Liska:63:102) Congress has also been willing to exercise its power of the purse through decreasing the Executive's request for foreign aid funds, by as much as forty-six percent (46%). (See Table Two)

Congress has also influenced the decision making process by holding extensive hearings and forcing the Executive to submit unusually lengthy and detailed budgetary requests. (O'Leary:67:127) But, until the late 1960s the policy initiative was always the Executive's. By 1973 with the passage of the Basic Human Needs Amendment, which was adopted over the objections of the Office of Management and Budget, the initiative in foreign aid policy had shifted from the Executive to the Congress. (Pastor:80:278-279)

There are important empirical implications to the shift in policy initiative from the Executive to the Legislative branch. First, as noted in Chapter One, the passage of the 1973 Basic Human Needs Amendment may make a new foreign aid period. In addition, McKinlay and Little's and Kato's research are based on the allocation of foreign aid funds during the decade of the sixties. The empirical research utilizing data for the 1970's is limited to the analysis of United States Human Rights and Basic Human Needs policy. (see Chapter Two) Consequently, there has not been a comprehensive evaluation of the impact of the Congressional initiatives of the 1970s on the allocation of bilateral United States foreign aid.

In relation to the power setting of A.I.D., the implications are unclear. Tendler, who provides the most comprehensive evaluation of A.I.D.'s power relationships, published her analysis in 1975, and makes no mention of the Basic Human Needs Amendment or the impact of increased Congressional influence on A.I.D.. However, the shift in policy initiative has probably enhanced A.I.D.'s power setting by decreasing the influence of the Department of Treasury and Commerce, in effect making it more difficult to substitute their balance of payment and promotion of export policies for a Basic Human Needs policy.

However, this is speculation which is not empirically supported. The policy initiative by Congress weakened the Executive led coalition, but it did not eliminate Presidential control or influence. Foreign aid and A.I.D. remain relatively unpopular in Congress and among the American people. Morss and Morss, writing in 1982, concluded that the Executive has been forced to concede a significant level of decision making authority and control to the Congress, but the Executive remains more influential. (Morss & Morss:82:75) Ripley and Franklin, in 1984, classified development assistance as strategic policy concluding that the "executive tends to prevail when there is conflict." (Ripley & Franklin:84:100-101, 229) The primary impact of the Congressional initiatives of the 1970s may have been a reduction of A.I.D.'s budget allocations resulting from the weakening the Executive led coalition.

So far, this review of the foreign aid decision making process has stressed the differences between the President and Congress and has not stressed the differences between the Senate and House. However, Fenno, in his study on Congressmen and Committees , concluded that the House and the Senate vary significantly in relation to "size, procedure, constituency and tenure. They, in turn, combine to produce very different decision making structures in the two chambers." (Fenno:73:146) The difference between the two chambers, as noted by Fenno, has created distinctly different decision making goals and environments. Which in turn has affected each chamber's consideration of foreign aid policy.

The hypothesis that the decision making process of the House and Senate vary significantly can be tested by examining the foreign aid appropriation bills of each chamber, prior to conference. However, the primary research question is whether the Executive and the Congress vary significantly in there consideration of foreign aid policy.

If the difference is significant, than further investigation into the intra-institutional variance of the Legislative branch is justified. This hypothesis will not be tested. Still, testing the relationship between the Executive and Legislative branches, requires a consideration of the differences between chambers.

Because of the distinct constitutional prerogatives of two the chambers, the Senate has tended to stress foreign relations while the House has concentrated its activities on questions of appropriation. (Fenno:73:151) Partly as a result of the differences in policy emphasis, the Senate was the first chamber to significantly challenge the Executive lead coalition and propose significant changes in foreign aid policy. Fenno noted that the differences between the two chambers resulted in a more individualistic decision making process in the Senate as compared to the House. (Fenno:73:146) And it was an individual, Senator Fulbright, Chairman of the Senate Foreign Relations Committee, who first initiated major policy proposals that were resisted by A.I.D. and the Executive.

Senator Fulbright's actions appear to have been based on good policy motives. The Senator was a strong supporter of foreign aid and attempted to alter United States bilateral policy in an effort to improve its overall effectiveness.

Fulbright's first policy initiative was in the area of population control. A.I.D. during the early 1960s did not consider population growth to be a developmental problem, and consequently refused to support population related programs. Senator Fulbright was successful in gathering the necessary support in the Senate and, during conference with the House, to "pass an amendment which specifically authorized A.I.D. to support research and technical assistance in population control." (Pastor:80:273)

Fulbright also suggested, several times to A.I.D. and the President, that military and economic assistance be separated and considered as independent appropriation bills. In 1966, despite the fact that such action would result in intensifying the scrutiny of Vietnam aid, President Johnson accepted Fulbright's recommendation and, and beginning in 1969, submitted two foreign aid bills, one for economic assistance and a second appropriations bill for military assistance. (Pastor:80:274)

In other areas, Senator Fulbright's activities were not as successful. Concerned over the impact of the annual authorizations process on the effectiveness of bilateral foreign aid policy, he recommended increased budgetary allocations to multilateral agencies and the adoption of two year budgetary authorizations. Thorough both proposals were eventually adopted, initially they ran into stiff opposition from Senator Morris who maintained that they would weaken the role of Congress in foreign aid policy. (Pastor:80:273) Most of Senator Fulbright's efforts to reform United States foreign aid policy occurred during the early to mid 1960s. By the late 1960s the political environment changed significantly as the Congress in general, and the Senate in particular, became preoccupied with its opposition to the Vietnam War.

As resistance to the President's policies in Vietnam intensified, the Senate sought surrogates to express displeasure. One such surrogate became the annual foreign aid appropriations bill. (Pastor:80:274-275) As a consequence, for the first time in 1971 the Senate voted down the annual appropriations bill by a vote of twenty-seven to forty-one. The defeat was the result of an unusual coalition between conservatives, who historically have tended to be critical of United States foreign aid policies, and liberals objecting to the size and uses of the Security Assistance Program. But the failure to pass the annual appropriations bill was primarily the result of the Senate displeasure over the House's refusal to approve the Mansfield Amendment cutting off funds for the Vietnam War. (Pastor:80:278)

US Domestic Explanations

The use of the foreign aid appropriations bill as a surrogate for the antiwar mood of the Senate is an interesting illustration of a phenomenon noted by Fenno in his consideration of the Senate Foreign Relations Committee. The Senate is both proud and protective of its foreign relations prerogatives and wishes to actively participate in the decision making process through a special degree of Executive consultations. (Fenno:73:161-167) It should be noted that this is essentially the process adopted by President Truman when he engaged in extensive consultation with Senator Vandenberg as part of the foreign aid decision making process. (Crabb & Holt:84:58)

However, Fenno also noted a serious dissatisfaction with the foreign aid bill primarily because of the time the bill consumed. The Senate seemed to resent the bill as a distraction, consuming time which would have been more profitably spent in consideration of other areas of United States foreign policy. (Fenno:73:162-163) One consequence of this resentment may have been the willingness of the Committee and the Senate to use the annual foreign aid appropriations bill to gain additional influence over other areas of foreign policy, particularity concerning Vietnam.

The Senate refused to pass the foreign aid bill for three consecutive years, 1971-1973. During this time,

"A.I.D. usually functioned on the basis of continuing resolutions at existing levels of appropriations rather than by annual legislative mandate." (Pastor:80:278)

Prior to the early 1970s substantive challenges to the Executive led coalition were primarily concentrated in the Senate. During this period, the House led by the Foreign Affairs Committee formed an alliance with the Executive Branch. As noted by Fenno, the Foreign Affairs Committee Chairman, Representative Morgan, believed the House to be "the subordinate partner in a permanent alliance with the Executive Branch." (Fenno:73:71) The primary objective of the House Foreign Affairs Committee was to assist the President in passage of the foreign aid bill. (Fenno:73:69-73)

As a consequence of the alliance between the President and the House Foreign Affairs Committee, House conferees tended to support the President's position during conference with the Senate and challenged the policy initiatives of the Senate when conflict occurred. (Pastor:80:274) However, starting in "1970 the House began to make changes in long-cherished norms, [and began] to divorce itself from the Executive conduct of international affairs and simultaneously to revise its own operating process." (Whale:82:16-17) This shift in the House of Representatives was to have significant impact on foreign aid policy, and resulted in a shift in the policy impetus between the chambers of Congress.

By 1973 the new policy emphasis in the House resulted in a House led coalition which broke the Senate caused deadlock over the foreign aid appropriations bill, and led to the adoption of the Basic Human Needs Amendment to the Foreign Assistance Act of 1961. (Pastor:80:278/ Whale:82:59-62) The new initiative of the House caused the most dramatic shift in United States bilateral aid policy since the Korean War. Until 1973, the emphasis of United States foreign aid policy was a combination of an economic strategy designed to "maximize gross national product and industrialization, and a political strategy of providing the largest of aid and food commodities to military allies." (Pastor:80:278) The Basic Human Needs Amendment shifted the policy emphasis into new directions mandating "people oriented" projects designed to help the "poorest countries and the poorest sector of the population in those countries." (Pastor:80:278/ Whale:82:60)

The new policy initiative in the House was based primarily on the power of the purse. The House because of the size of foreign aid expenditures and the requirement for annual appropriations, has been able to use the foreign aid bill as an "opportunity to write international policy."

(Whale:82:81) The shift in policy emphasis from the Senate to the House continued through the 1970s as the House proposed additional measures designed to shape the foreign aid policy of the United States. Of particular importance are the amendments limiting the allocation of United States foreign aid to regimes and governments which continue to engage in gross violations of recognized human rights. The first such measure was passed in 1974 as a joint effort of both chambers. The 1974 amendment limited the allocation of security assistance monies, "except in extraordinary circumstances" to countries with "gross violations of internationally recognized human rights." (Crabb & Holt:84:193)

The next year the House reasserted its new found influence with the introduction of House Bill 9005, which barred all forms of foreign aid to countries violating human rights except for aid designed to help the most needy portion of the recipient state's population. (Whale:82:123) The House again expressed its concerns of human rights in 1976 when the 1974 amendment was strengthened with the intent of terminating all security assistance to countries that violated human rights. (Whale:82:122)

The long term effects of the House measures in the field of foreign policy and foreign aid is a matter of conjecture.

US Domestic Explanations

The human rights amendments in particular are weakened in that the President of the United States is usually provided some level of discretionary powers to continue the flow of foreign aid under extraordinary circumstances, or if the human rights record of the recipient state in question showed improvement. The foreign aid literature considered in Chapter Two concerning basic human needs and human rights suggest that the change in policy may have been more cosmetic than substantive. However, as long as the Executive must rely on the exchange of economic resources as a instrument of international policy, the Congress will continue to have the potential of significant influence.

CONCLUSIONS

The primary objective of this chapter is to outline the domestic foreign aid decision making process, for those domestic institutions with substantive decision making authority. Considering the nature of the decision making process within the Executive Branch, it is unreasonable to separate A.I.D. decisions from those of its rival agencies. This is largely a consequence of research design rather than the inability of political research methodology to distinguish between the activities A.I.D. and the other Executive Agencies involved in foreign aid decision making process.

US Domestic Explanations

Unraveling the inter agency decision making process requires the appropriate research methodology. The most appropriate methodology would be the use of extensive interviews and personal observations to determine the relative position and influence of each actor in the Executive decision making process. The research design and techniques utilized by Judith Tendler and Richard Fenno are examples of an appropriate research methodology capable of identifying the relative influences of each participant in a complex decision making environment with many actors. (Tendler:75/Fenno:73)

The research techniques and methodologies being utilized by this study are incapable of making this distinction. Consequently, the Executive Branch will be considered as a unitary decision making unit, and the Presidential budgetary request will be operationalized as the Executive Branch dependent variable. However, it is recognized that the dependent variable is the outcome of a complex inter agency decision making process which results in a compromise between A.I.D., the President and other Executive Departments.

The domestic literature and the examples noted appear to indicate that the President plays an unusually significant role in foreign aid funding decisions. As a consequence, there is the potential for individual Presidential leadership and policy priorities to significantly affect the allocation of bilateral foreign aid. To test this hypothesis, it would be necessary to subdivide the temporal period by Presidential term. Separate analysis would then be made for each administration, and the results compared to determine the relative influence of Presidential leadership. While this question is of interest, it is of secondary importance to the primary research question. Consequently, the research question of Presidential leadership is a matter for future study.

The literature review clearly supports the hypothesis that the foreign aid decision making processes, and policy priorities, vary significantly between the Executive and Legislative branches. It is relatively easy to separate the foreign aid decisions of the Executive and Congress, since each must act independently on foreign aid expenditures. The executive through the request for funds, and the legislative through the annual foreign aid appropriations bill. The differences across domestic institutions with legal constitutional authority is the primary research focus of this analysis. To test this question, the Executive request and the final version of the foreign aid bill, will be operationalized as dependent variables and tested independently. The results of each analysis will be compared to determine the relative influence of each in the allocation of United States economic foreign aid administered by A.I.D..

TABLE TWO

DIFFERENCE BETWEEN FOREIGN ASSISTANCE FUNDS REQUESTED BY THE EXECUTIVE AND CONGRESSIONAL APPROPRIATIONS AND AUTHORIZATIONS FOR SELECTED YEARS YEAR

REQUESTI	APPROPRIATIONS	AUTHORIZATIONS	DIFFERENCE
1950	5.68	4.94	5.59
1952	8.50	7.28	7.58
1954	5.83	4.53	5.16
1956	3.53	2.70	3.42
1958	3.86	2.77	3.39
1960	3.93	3.23	3.58
1962	4.77	3.91	4.26
1964	4.53	3.0	3.60
1966	3.46	3.22	3.36
1968	3.23	2.30	2.68
1970	2.21	1425*	
1971	2.008	1.734*	

* (Chunningham:74:85: source does not report authorizations)
(Pastor:80:255-256)

FIGURE NUMBER NINE

THE RELATIVE IMPORTANCE OF INSTITUTIONAL DECISION MAKING RELATIONSHIPS THAT DETERMINE THE ALLOCATION OF FOREIGN AID A COMPARISON OF THE FOOD FOR PEACE AND ECONOMIC ASSISTANCE PROGRAMS

PART ONE:
FOOD FOR PEACE
(structural policy decisions)

```
 ________________                            ____________
I President &    I                          I            I
I Centralized    I* * * * * * * * * * * * * I  Congress  I
I Bureaucracy    I                          I____________I
I________________I                                *
        *                                         *
        *                                         *
        *                                         *
        *                                         *
        *                                         *
        *                                         *
 _______*________                         ________*_______
I                 I                       I    Bureaus     I
I Sub-CommitteesI IxxxxxxxxxxxxxxxxxxxxxxxI(Dept. of Ag.)  I
I_________________I                       I________________I
                   x                     x
                    x                   x
                     x                 x
                      x               x
                       x             x
                        x           x
                         x         x
                          x       x
                           x     x
                            x   x
                             x x
                        ______x______
                       I Private Sector I
                       I (AG & Farm IG) I
                       I________________I
```

Very Important Relationship = x x x x x x x x x x x x x
Moderately Important Relationship = # # # # # # # # # #
Relatively Unimportant Relationships = * * * * * * * * * *
(Ripley & Franklin:84:242 & 243)

FIGURE NUMBER NINE

THE RELATIVE IMPORTANCE OF INSTITUTIONAL DECISION MAKING RELATIONSHIPS THAT DETERMINE THE ALLOCATION OF FOREIGN AID A COMPARISON OF THE FOOD FOR PEACE AND ECONOMIC ASSISTANCE PROGRAMS

PART TWO;
OTHER FORMS OF ECONOMIC A.I.D.
(strategic policy decisions)

```
 ________________________                       __________
I                        I                     I          I
IPresident & Centralized Ix x x x x x x   x x xI Congress I
I     Bureaucracy        I                     I__________I
I________________________I                    #
                  #                          #
                    #                      #
                      #                  #
                        #              #
                          #          #
                            #      #
 ___________                  #  #                _____________
I           I                 #  #               I             I
I  Bureaus  I* * * * * * * * * *#* * *   * * **I Sub-         I
I (A.I.D.)  I                  #                I CommitteessI
I___________I*                 #                I_____________I
               *               #               *
                 *             #             *
                   *           #           *
                     *         #         *
                       *  _____#______ *
                         I            I
                         I Private Sector I
                         I   (I.G.)   I
                         I____________I
```

Very Important Relationship = x x x x x x x x x x x x x
Moderately Important Relationship = # # # # # # # # # #
Relatively Unimportant Relationships = * * * * * * * * * *
(Ripley & Franklin:84:242 & 243)

CHAPTER FOUR

RESEARCH DESIGN AND METHODOLOGY

> "A model has three major elements; a set of components variables, a hypothesis relating these variables, and a rationale that underlines and explains this relationship" (McKinlay and Little:77:59)

The review of the international and domestic literature has outlined several potential explanations for the allocation of United States foreign aid. However, the literature provides limited information as to the validity of each potential explanation or of the relative relationship between explanations, across domestic institutions. To test the validity of the propositions found in the literature and to identify the relative explanatory power of the competing explanations, it is necessary to specify a research design consisting of four basic elements:

1. a conceptual framework to provide the necessary theoretical and research parameters to guide the research process;
2. a set of hypotheses derived from the analytical conceptual framework;

3. a set of indicators to capture and measure phenomenon and relationships of interest; and
4. a research methodology that is capable of reliably testing the hypotheses derived from the conceptual framework.

Some portion of each these elements has previously been described in the literature reviewed. The task here, is to consider these elements in more depth and bring them together in a comprehensive research design. The research design will be constructed from its for elements, starting with its conceptual framework and adding the other elements in their turn.

ANALYTIC SCHEME

> "It is beneficial to approach the topics of international relations with some systematic conceptual scheme. One such analytical scheme is the rational decision concept." (Kato:69:198)

An analytic scheme consists of several research parameters and theoretical constructs which give structure and guidance to the research process. For this research project, the analytical scheme must integrate the basic premises and propositions of the international and domestic approaches to explaining United States bilateral foreign aid allocations. Fortunately, the two approaches share the theoretical parameters of the rational choice paradigm, which makes their integration a relatively easy task.

The rational choice paradigm is the most common analytical scheme utilized to explain the allocation of foreign aid. For this reason, and because the rational choice paradigm is adopted as the main component of the research design for this project, it is pertinent to consider the assumptions of the paradigm in relation to foreign aid decision making in some detail. In this manner, the theoretical similarities and distinctions between the international and domestic approaches can be illustrated, as well as integrated, into a single analytical scheme.

There are four theoretical constructs, concerning the allocation of United States foreign aid, that are necessary to meet the basic theoretical parameters of the rational choice paradigm. The first construct, necessary to operationalize the rational choice paradigm, is the identification of a specific decision making unit. The definition of the decision making unit is also the primary variance between the domestic and international approaches to explaining foreign aid allocations.

Research Design

For the international approach, the decision making unit is defined as the donor state. The donor state is conceived as the "decision making unit which is responsible for the entire process of allocating foreign aid." (Kato:69:199) The premise of the international approach is that the donor state decides how much aid to allocate to each recipient state based on specified salient characteristics of the recipient state. Whether these salient characteristics are military, economic, or humanitarian depends on the hypothetical relationship being tested. However, for both the foreign policy and recipient needs explanation, it is assumed that the donor state, not domestic institutions or the recipient state, is the decision making unit of interest.

In contrast, the domestic approach adopts the intrastate institutions of the donor state as the decision making units of interest; in effect rejecting Kato's definition as a single decision making unit responsible for the allocation of foreign aid. The premise of the domestic approach is that the allocation of bilateral foreign aid is the result of a compromise between donor state institutions with legal-constitutional authority over foreign aid expenditures.

This institutional competition is partly the result of varying priorities and policy perspectives across institutions, but is also the result of differences in the political environment across institutions. However, a significant portion of the competition is the result of each institution attempting to increase or maintain influence over foreign aid policy and the allocation of foreign aid monies.

Both the international and domestic specification of the decision making units represent an over simplification of reality. Both approaches fail to consider the recipient state as an important decision maker in the foreign aid allocation process. Certain third world states, such as Burma, have rejected most forms of assistance from virtually all potential donors. Other third world states have limited, or have tightly controlled, both the form and amount of assistance they will accept.

Consequently, the explanatory power of any rational choice model utilizing the donor state, or its institutions, as the sole decision making unit have limited explanatory potential. However, the inclusion of the recipient state as a decision making unit greatly increases the complexity of the analysis, and while the failure to consider the recipient state represents an over simplification of reality, it is not the intent of this research project to extend the empirical research found in the literature to include consideration of the recipient state as a decision making unit.

Kato's adoption of the donor state as the decision making unit includes a second over simplification of reality in that it suppresses any potential variance across domestic institutions that influence foreign aid allocations. The question is whether the observable allocation of foreign aid across recipient states is a result of a unitary decision maker (the donor state), or the result of a compromise between intrastate decision makers and institutions, that vary in their foreign aid policy priorities and decision making environments.

The primary research objective of this study is to extend our understanding of the foreign aid allocation process through the operationalization of empirical models designed to capture the differences across intrastate institutions that have legal-constitutional authority over foreign aid expenditures. Consequently, there are two decision making units of interest, the Executive and Congress. Both decision making units will be considered separately, and the results compared to determine the preferences and priorities of each.

Research Design

The second premise of the rational choice paradigm is that the decision making unit has a set of goals ranked in hierarchical order based on the relative utility of the decision maker. (Holt & Turner:76) Because of the first assumption, that the decision making units of interest are the institutions of the donor state, the set of decision making goals is reflective of the donor state's preferences. The research question of interest is whether the decision making goals and utility vary across the institutions of the donor state.

The decision making goals of the donor state include the seven foreign aid decision making strategies, derived from the international approach found in the literature, and presented in Chapter Two:

1. The security containment strategy stipulates that the decision making goals of the donor state is to promote and protect its national security interests.
2. The geopolitical power strategy stipulates that the decision making goal of the donor state is to promote positive relations with recipient states that have a substantial geopolitical power potential.
3. The economic self interest strategy stipulates that the decision making goal of the donor state is to protect and promote its own economic interest.

4. The development strategy stipulates that the decision making goal of the donor state is to promote the economic development of the recipient state to encourage the formation of free market economies that are consistent with the economic ideologies and structure of the donor state.
5. The political ideology strategy stipulates that the decision making goal of the donor state is to promote the development of regimes that are ideologically consistent with the political system of the donor state.
6. The systemic stability strategy stipulates that the decision making goal of the donor state is to promote the political stability of the recipient state to protect the donor state's self interest, and to maintain the stability of the international system.
7. The humanitarian strategy stipulates that the decision making goal of the donor state is to improve the recipients the quality of life of by addressing the basic human needs of the recipient state's population.

The question is which policy objective has the greatest utility, or represents the most appropriate foreign aid policy, for the donor state. Because the international approach adopts the donor state as the sole decision making unit, the political impact of institutional goals is not a consideration.

In contrast, the domestic approach tends to stress the goals of intrastate institutions. The primary institutional goal is the maintenance and/or expansion of influence over foreign aid policies and budget. Through foreign aid policy, both the Executive and Legislative branches can pursue international policy objectives and control, and influence, several billion dollars of expenditures.

In the competition for influence, the Executive coalition led by the President appears to have an advantage. However, the Congress, as illustrated in Chapter Three, is not without influence particularly in regards to appropriations.

In addition to institutional goals, the domestic approach recognizes that the goals of individual participants, taken collectively, can affect foreign aid allocations. To illustrate this point, it is helpful to consider Richard Fenno's observations concerning individual member goals reported in his book Congressmen in Committee.

Fenno studied the committees responsible for the authorization of foreign aid expenditures, and the appropriation committees which must approve actual foreign aid expenditures. Properly modified, and combined with material from other sources, Fenno's observations can help define and clarify the policy goals of both Congress and the Executive.

For both authorization committees (the Senate Foreign Relations Committee and the House Foreign Affairs Committee), Fenno identified good policy as the primary member goal.* (Fenno:73:9-14, 141-142) An example of the pursuit of the good foreign aid policy goal of Congress are the acts of Senator Fullbright, and the Congressional adoption of the basic human needs and basic human rights criteria during the early to mid seventies.

The relative explanatory power of the good policy goal in relation to the explanatory power of the Congressional institutional influence goal is an important research question for this analysis. However, for the specification of the analytical scheme, it is adequate to assume that a significant portion of the Congressional foreign aid policy decision making is based on good policy considerations.

---

*Fenno uses the term "good policy" to refer to individual and organizational goals that are not influenced by personal or organizational considerations of self interest.

Research Design

For the House and Senate appropriation committees, Fenno identified chamber influence as the primary member goal. When generalized to the institutional level, member influence becomes Congressional influence which has already been discussed as an important foreign aid decision making goal. However, in addition to member influence, Fenno identified reelection and good policy as secondary goals.

The relative import of these secondary goals vary between the Senate and House, but there is support for expanding both decision making goals to the institutional level. First, the importance of the reelection goal and the ability to serve constituent interests was recognized by Agency for International Development when the agency adopted the policy of informing each Senator and Representative of domestic foreign aid expenditures by state and Congressional district. (Morss & Morss:82:81)

In addition, in McKinlay and Little's findings, there is evidence that the allocation of foreign aid monies is significantly altered during election years. More specifically, the economic interest and the developmental interest decision making strategies have increased saliency during election years. (McKinlay & Little:79:249) (See Table Three) Based on this evidence and Fenno's observations, the reelection goal appears to have saliency when generalized from the appropriations committees to the Congress as a whole. The good policy goal of the appropriations committees can also be generalized to the institutional level. But, the definition of what constitutes good policy varies between the appropriations and authorization committees.

During the appropriation process foreign aid funds, as noted in Chapter Three, are in competition with domestic and military programs. This budgetary competition for limited resources can manifest itself as a good budgetary policy goal that is independent of the bilateral relationship between donor and recipient states but, nevertheless, effects the allocation of United States bilateral foreign aid. According to budgetary theory, the competition for scarce funds is partly dependent upon the state of the United States economy. If the economy is expanding, the pool of available resources increases and the competition for those resources decreases. The hypothesized result is increased funding for the foreign aid program. This phenomena is operationalized as a domestic economic policy goal, and is added to the analytic scheme, at the institutional level.

Research Design

To some extent the reelection and domestic economy goals are complementary. In that, the competition for budgetary allocations is most intense during election years as Senators and Representatives attempt to allocate funds to satisfy their constituencies and in response to interest group pressure. Noting the general lack of public support for the foreign aid program, one would assume that the foreign aid budget would tend to decline during election years.

In addition, Congress might be expected to shift foreign aid funds across programs and policy objectives. Not all foreign aid programs or policies are equally supported or disliked by the American public. The Food for Peace Program, for example, enjoys strong support from agricultural interests and there is general support among the American public for an ideologically based foreign aid policy. In response to reelection pressures, Congress might shift funds from programs with limited interest group and popular support to those programs that enjoy greater support among the American public and interest groups.

There are a total of ten operationalized decision making goals identified in the international and domestic literature that are adopted for the analytic scheme. Seven of these goals are derived from the international approach and represent good foreign aid policy goals. Three goals are derived from the domestic approach which include:

1. The good budgetary and domestic economic policy goal which stipulates that the funds available for foreign aid depends partly on the economic condition of the United States and on the competition with domestic and military programs for limited budgetary funds.
2. The reelection goal which stipulates that the decision making unit will alter foreign aid allocations during election years in a manner designed to enhance individual reelection.
3. The institutional influence goal which stipulates that the allocation of foreign aid is affected by the competition between institutions attempting to maintain or increase their control or influence over foreign aid policy and budget.

While the domestic goals have been presented within the context of the Legislative branch, they will also be adopted to explain the decision making behavior of the Executive branch. Whether each decision making goal is significant for both institutions is a matter for empirical testing. However, to determine the relative import of each goal and to provide consistent results for cross institutional comparisons, it is necessary to apply identical analytic schemes to each institution and compare the empirical results. Consequently, the seven international policy goals and the three domestic goals are adopted for both the Executive and Legislative branches.

No rationale has been given provided for two of the independent variables that comprise the domestic model, and it is appropriate to do so now. The multilateral aid independent variable recognizes that the United States annually donates substantial sums to international organizations which administer multilateral aid; including the distribution of multilateral aid to many of the recipients of United States bilateral aid. The rationale behind the indicator is basically a budgetary policy question.

If a given recipient state requires $100 million dollars of economic aid, and is receiving $50 million dollars from the World Bank or some other multilateral source, then it is good budgetary policy for the United States to limit its bilateral foreign aid allocations to $50 million dollars. To provide more than $50 million dollars would be wasteful in that the recipient state would receive more aid than its total need.

The second indicator is designed to test the impact of domestic agricultural interest on the allocation of United States bilateral aid. While the indicator is designed primarily to test the hypothetical relationship between donor state agricultural interest groups and the Food for Peace Program, the indicator will also be regressed against the Executive request and the Congressional appropriations for Agency for International Development economic aid.

The third assumption necessary to operationalize the rational choice paradigm is that the decision making unit has a series of alternatives that are ranked according to the goal preferences of the second assumption, and the decision maker "always chooses the highest ranked alternative." (Gordon:82:238) In this manner, the decision making unit attempts to maximize its utility by allocating scarce foreign aid funds to those recipient states that add "the greatest increment of values to the decision maker." (Kato:69:200) In addition, it is assumed that the decision maker will be consistent; in that when faced with the same set of alternatives the highest ranked alternative will always be selected, all things being equal. (Gordon:82:238)

The relative consistency of foreign aid decisions has important implications for Kato's assumption that the donor state is a unitary decision making unit. If the empirical evidence suggests that the institutions involved in foreign aid decisions consistently select funding alternatives that reflect a single set of rank order preferences, with equal explanatory power, then it is reasonable to assume that there is a general consensus concerning foreign aid policy across domestic institutions, adding validity to Kato's assumption and the international approach.

However, if there is evidence of inconsistent decisions, or if foreign aid funding decisions reflect more than one set of rank order preferences across institutions, then one can hypothesize that the final allocation of foreign aid is the result of a composite measure of relative utility. The adoption of a composite measure of relative utility can be interpreted as the result of a compromise between domestic decision makers with competing rank order preferences. This would strengthen the domestic approach to explaining the allocation of United States bilateral foreign aid.

The fourth, and final, assumption is that the decision maker "knows the probable consequence of choosing each alternative." (Gordon:82:238) In relation to foreign aid, this requires adequate "information of the state of the world." (Kato:69:200) However, the international system is dynamic and in a constant state of flux. Because of the dynamic nature of the international system, it is probable that the actual pattern of foreign aid allocations will vary over time as the conditions of specific recipient states, the domestic economy of the donor state, and the political environment of domestic institutions change.

Foreign aid decisions, therefore, depend in part on the specific state of the world for a given temporal period. The current allocation of foreign aid for time (t) is largely based on the state of the world for the previous year (t-1). "This means that only the previous year's events affect the information relevant to the allocation process of aid." (Kato:69:200) However, according to Wildavski, the budgetary process takes approximately eighteen months, and there is supporting evidence in the foreign aid literature that foreign aid decisions take from fifteen to nineteen months. (Wildavski:84/Morss & Morss:82:84/ Nelson:68:57)

As a consequence, it may be appropriate to assume that foreign aid allocation decisions are based on the condition of the world two years prior to the actual allocation decision. To reflect this possibility, it is necessary to operationalize two sets of models, one based on the previous year's state of the world (t-1) and a second set of models based on the state of the world two years prior to the allocation decision (t-2). (Kato:69:200) However, Kato, who tested this hypothesis, determined that military aid is more affected by the two year time lag than economic aid. Consequently, there appears to be limited cause to operationalize a two year lag as part of the research design. (see Table Three)

The rational choice paradigm is the primary component of the analytical scheme. However, further consideration of the foreign aid phenomenon is necessary to complete the analytical scheme. Foreign aid is a complex phenomenon, partly because there is not one foreign aid program, administrative agency, or policy. Rather, there is a set of programs each having its own authorization legislation and allocation criteria. The result is a complex set of policies and decision making goals, which may or may not, be coordinated across programs.

The implicit assumption of McKinlay and Little's research, as illustrated in Chapter Three, is that the differences across programs is unimportant because the donor state utilizes all foreign aid monies to achieve a single set of policy objectives. However, this implicit assumption is rejected for this research project. In its place, it is assumed that the different foreign aid programs are designed to achieve different foreign aid policy objectives, and that the allocation pattern varies across programs. This assumption will be tested as a secondary research question in Chapter Five. Given this assumption, to complete the analytical scheme, it is necessary to specify the foreign aid program of interest.

Based on Kato's conclusions concerning military and economic aid, it is reasonable to separate the two forms of aid and consider them separately. However, economic aid includes the activities of four basic programs and at least three agencies, including; the Agency for International Development, the Peace Corps, some activities of the Import-Export Bank, and the Food for Peace Program which is jointly administered by the Department of Agriculture and Agency for International Development. Of these four programs, only economic aid administered by Agency for International Development, excluding the security assistance program, is being considered.

To provide some indication of the potential differences across foreign aid programs, the results of this research will be compared to the conclusions of McKinlay and Little. Such a comparison is incomplete however, because McKinlay and Little attempt to explain total foreign aid allocations and make no distinctions between programs or military and economic aid. Still, if there is a significant difference between the Agency for International Development's allocations and total allocations, one can assume that the variance is caused by the impact of military aid. In addition, the allocations of the Food for Peace Program will be compared to the allocation of Agency for International Development funds. However, this is a secondary research question and there is no intent of providing an intensive analysis of the potential variance across foreign aid programs.

HYPOTHESES AND PROPOSITIONS

The second element of the research design is a set of hypotheses, suggested by the analytical scheme, that are reflective of the causal relationship being tested. As noted the primary research question, and therefore the basic hypothesis, of this research project is to test for the differences in the foreign aid decision making determinants between the Executive and Congress. However, to test this hypothesis, it is necessary to operationalize several additional hypotheses that capture the underlying causes for the variance in the decision making determinants across domestic institutions.

The causal relationships being tested are structured by the rational choice paradigm. The basic premises of the paradigm is that decisions are the result, or are caused by, the decision makers' pursuit of identifiable goals. In the case of foreign aid policy, these goals include the seven international policy goals and three domestic goals outlined in the analytic scheme. The basic premises is that the allocation of foreign aid is caused by the Executive and Legislative pursuit of these goals.

In addition to the basic hypotheses and the related propositions, a number of secondary research questions were noted in the literature review. As secondary research questions, these propositions are not necessary to test the validity of the primary research question. Rather, they raise related questions pertaining to the allocation of foreign aid which can be pursued in future research. Most of the secondary research questions have been noted but will not be investigated further. The only secondary questions that will be investigated are the variance across foreign aid programs, and whether the basic human needs amendment of 1973 mark a new foreign aid period.

Formally stated, the basic hypothesis being investigated is that the budgetary request of the Executive, supported by the Executive led coalition, is the primary determining factor in the allocation of United States bilateral economic aid as administered by Agency for International Development. This hypothesis stresses the dominant role of the Executive branch for two reasons. First, the domestic literature reviewed in Chapter Three clearly indicates that an Executive led coalition dominates United States foreign aid policy.

The second reason for operationalizing the basic hypothesis in relation to the Executive branch is the causal sequence of the budgetary process. The Executive submits its budgetary request for funds to the Congress which, after due consideration, responds in the form of an appropriations bill. The basic research question is whether there is significant variance between domestic institutions with legal constitutional authority over foreign aid decisions. However, given the strong support for the Executive led coalition in the domestic literature and the causal sequence of the budgetary process, it is appropriate to operationalize this proposition in reference to the Executive.

To test this proposition, it is necessary to operationalize nine additional hypotheses to capture the decision making goals of the analytic scheme:

1. Recipient Needs Hypothesis; the distribution of bilateral economic foreign aid is proportional to the humanitarian and basic human needs of the recipient state.

2. Security Interest Hypothesis; the distribution of bilateral economic foreign aid is proportional to the security interest of the donor state.
3. Geopolitical Power Hypothesis; the distribution of bilateral economic foreign aid is proportional to the potential geopolitical power of the recipient state.
4. Political Ideology Hypothesis; the distribution of bilateral economic foreign aid is proportional to the ideological consistency between the donor and recipient state.
5. Stability Interest Hypothesis; the distribution of bilateral economic foreign aid is proportional to the level of political instability of the recipient state's regime.
6. Development Interest Hypothesis; the distribution of bilateral economic foreign aid is proportional to the recipient state's potential for economic development.
7. Economic Self Interest Hypothesis; the distribution of bilateral economic foreign aid is proportional to the economic self interest of the donor state.
8. Domestic Economy Hypothesis; the domestic economy of the donor state has an effect on the distribution of bilateral economic aid.
9. Reelection Hypothesis; the distribution of bilateral economic aid is affected by the reelection goals of

individuals which has a collective effect on domestic institutions altering the allocation of foreign aid.

Each of these hypotheses will be tested against the preferred foreign aid allocation pattern of the Executive and Legislative branches. In this manner, the preference of each branch can be determined and compared across domestic institutions.

RESEARCH METHODOLOGY

> "However, conclusions . . . can only be reliably inferred from the data if the estimation procedure is appropriate and if the variables selected as proxies for ±donor interest' and ±recipient needs' are good proxies." (Mosley:81:246)

Kato and McKinlay and Little adopt the same basic research design to explain the allocation of bilateral foreign aid. Each specifies several sets of distinct independent variables designed to capture different propositions, and adopt foreign aid expenditures as their dependent variables.

Research Design

To test their propositions and hypothesized relationships, Kato and McKinlay and Little apply multiple regression analysis and ordinary least squares statistical techniques to measure and compare the relative validity of the foreign aid decision making strategies and hypotheses operationalized. The same basic research methodology is adopted to test the ten hypotheses presented. However, unlike Kato's and McKinlay and Little's research, the unit of analysis under consideration is the Executive and Congress. Consequently, it is necessary to alter and extend Kato's and McKinlay and Little's research methodology.

The basic research methodology is to operationalize the Executive branch's request for funds and Congressional appropriations as the dependent variables. To explain the variance in the dependent variables across recipient states, several models, designed to capture the foreign aid decision making goals of the analytical scheme, are operationalized and regressed against the dependent variables. In this manner, the transitive relationship of the foreign aid decision making determinants can be identified for each institution. By comparing the similarities and differences in the transitive rank order preferences, it will be possible to determine the variance in foreign aid decision making determinants across domestic institutions.

Research Design

However, it must also be remembered that there is a relationship between the funding request of the Executive branch and the final appropriations of the Legislative branch. As noted, the legislature does not develop an independent foreign aid proposal. Rather, the Congress responds to and alters the proposals of the Executive branch. If the degree of variance between the Executive request and the Legislative action is insignificant, then it must be assumed that the Executive coalition is the primary decision maker, and the basic hypothesis will be rejected.

To determine whether the variance between the Executive request and Congressional appropriations is significant, the Executive request is regressed against the Congressional appropriations in a bivariant regression model. The Executive request is operationalized as the independent variable because of the causal sequence of the budgetary process.

It is assumed that the Executive request will explain a significant portion of Congressional appropriations, but that the unexplained portion of the model will be adequate to accept the primary hypothesis. However, significant variance does not necessarily mean that the two institutions vary in their foreign aid policy goals or decision making determinants.

Research Design

Several researchers have noted that Congress tends to reduce the Executive's foreign aid budget request. Consequently, it is feasible that the institutions are in agreement on the preferred pattern of foreign aid allocations, but differ in the level of aid to be allocated to each recipient state. This conclusion would tend to support the domestic economic interest hypothesis. If Congressional cuts in the Executive budget proposal are proportional across recipient states, the primary hypothesis will be rejected. To accept the hypothesis that the two institutions vary significantly in their decision making determinants, it is necessary that the rank order and/or explanatory power of the foreign aid decision making goals vary significantly across the Executive and Legislative branches.

To determine the explanatory power and rank order of the seven foreign aid policy goals derived from the international explanation, seven empirical models will be operationalized. Each model will be independently regressed against the dependent variables using cross sectional by year multiple regression and ordinary least squares statistical techniques.

There are two potential methodological difficulties that must be addressed. The first potential difficulty was previously noted in Chapter Two, simultaneous causation resulting from a relationship between the level of foreign aid and the GNP or GDP of the recipient state. As noted, to avoid the potential for simultaneous causation, the level of bilateral aid is removed from the independent variable GDP.

However, the model operationalized to measure the economic self interest of the donor state includes three measures related to GDP: 1) mining as a percent of GDP, 2) manufacturing as a percent of GDP, and 3) agriculture as a percent of GDP. Since it is not possible to determine the relationship between the level of aid and a specific economic activity, no corrective action can be taken. Consequently, the potential for a simultaneous causal relationship must be acknowledged. However, it seems unlikely that any such relationship will be strong enough to cause serious results. (Pindick and Rubinfeld:81: 152-161, 191-199)

The second potential methodological problem is the potential for a heteroscedastic relationship. The source of the heteroscedastic problem stems from the variance in the size of recipient states. It is quite possible that the error terms associated with large recipient states, such as India, will have larger variances than the error terms of smaller recipient states, such as Jamaica.

Research Design

To test for heteroscedasticity, the error terms will be converted into absolute values and regressed against the independent variables. If the resulting statistics indicate a significant relationship, corrective action, namely the adoption of weighted least squares statistical techniques, will be taken. To test for heteroscedasticity it is not necessary to test each model for each year. It is adequate to test a random sample, and if no relationship between the absolute value of the error terms and the independent variables is found, it will be assumed that variance of the error terms is consistent across cases. (Pindick & Rubinfeld:81:140-152)

The values of the independent variables operationalized to test the seven foreign aid strategies derived from the international explanation vary across recipient states. Consequently, there is no difficulty in testing the validity of these models for each year of the temporal period; and the number of cases for each year is adequate to support the number of independent variables being regressed against the dependent variables for each model. Unfortunately, this is not the case for the domestic model.

The domestic economic and reelection models measure characteristics of the donor state for each year of the temporal period. Consequently, the value of the independent variables across the recipient states are constant for each given year. The number of cases is dependent on the number of years under consideration rather than the number of recipient states. The cross sectional by year format utilized to test the international policy models is no longer appropriate. For the domestic indicators, pooled time series regression techniques are more appropriate.

The use of pooling techniques is valid only when the assumptions concerning the error term of the regression model are valid. Of particular concern is the potential for heteroscedasticity, colinearity, and auto correlation. As previously stated, the explanatory models will be tested for heteroscedasticity. The potential for a relationship between the independent variables, or colinearity, is particularly a concern for the domestic economic model. Because the independent variables of the model attempt to measure the level of donor state economic activity, it is reasonable to assume that there will be a linear relationship between the independent variables. To prevent colinearity, the indicators will be independently regressed against all the other independent variables.

Of the potential difficulties to using pooled time series analysis, auto correlation is the most likely. Auto correlation stems from the potential relationship between the error terms of one time period correlated with the error terms of a future time period. Given the nature of the indicators for the donor state economic activity model, it seems reasonable to assume that the error terms be correlated across time periods.

Auto correlation, however, affects the efficiency of the ordinary least squares regression estimator, but not their biasness or consistency. The presence of auto correlation weakens the explanatory power of the model in that the estimators will be smaller than the true standard error. As a result, there will be a tendency to reject the null hypothesis when it should be accepted, causing a type I error. The Durbin-Watson statistic will be used to test for auto correlation. (Pindick & Rubinfeld:81:87-90, 152-154, 158-161, 252-253)

INDICATORS AND MEASURES

> "The level of measurement that can be achieved is not inherent in the thing being measured, but it is a function of our ability to conceptualize." (Palumbo:69:11)

To test the validity of the propositions presented, it is necessary to operationalize indicators to measure the relative strength of the hypothesized causal relationships. To guide in the selection of indicators, two decision rules were adopted. The first decision rule was to replicate McKinlay and Little's indicators where methodologically appropriate. As noted in Chapter Two, there are specification problems with McKinlay and Little's recipient need and political stability and democracy models. These issues have already been addressed and will not be reviewed further; however, the necessary adjustments to the indicators are included in the appropriate models.

The second decision rule is to use continuous measures rather than dummy variables when feasible and appropriate. Dummy variables can provide significant insight when the value being measured is either present or absent. Election year is an excellent example of the appropriate use of dummy variables, it is either an election year or it is not.

However, McKinlay and Little utilize dummy variables to measure some indicators where continuous levels are available, such as the level of United States military assistance and arm sales to recipient states. For these indicators, it is more appropriate to assume that decision makers consider both the presence and the level of activity. Dummy variables are only capable of measuring the presence or absence, consequently, continuous measures appear more appropriate.

THE DEPENDENT VARIABLES

To measure the effects of Congressional consideration on the Executive request for foreign aid funds, the indicator adopted is the final appropriations for Agency for International Development economic assistance, excluding the security assistance program. The Congressional dependent variable was used to define the data set, and it should be noted that not every state receiving United States bilateral aid received assistance through Agency for International Development.

Israel is an example of a state that receives substantial bilateral foreign aid throughout the temporal period; however, Israel is not included in the data set because the aid extended was either military assistance or administered under the security assistance program. Consequently, the data set represents a subset of all recipients of United States bilateral aid for the temporal period.

The Executive budgetary request is operationalized to capture the foreign aid allocation preferences of the

Executive. However, this indicator was not available throughout the temporal period. A more detailed discussion of the executive request is provided in The Research Notes.

THE RECIPIENT NEED MODEL

The recipient needs model consists of six indicators, two are derived from McKinlay and Little's research and the remaining four are derived from the research of Hicks and Streeten. The two indicators derived from McKinlay and Little measure the economic need of the recipient state, while the remaining four indicators measure the basic human condition.

1. The balance of payments of the recipient state.
2. The gross population of the recipient state.
3. Calorie intake as a percentage of total daily requirements.
4. Infant mortality rate measured as the number of deaths per one thousand births.
5. Life expectancy at birth.
6. Per capita gross national product.

Research Design

THE SECURITY INTEREST MODEL

The Security Interest Model is operationalized with ten indicators to measure the bilateral security relationship between the recipient state, and the United States, and the Union of Soviet Socialist Republics. In addition, the model includes indicators to measure the economic relationship between Union of Soviet Socialist Republics and the recipient state.

1. The gross level of the United States military assistance.
2. The presence of United States bases, troops, military technicians, or military advisors operationalized as a dummy variable.
3. The gross level of United States arms transfers including subsidized and nonsubsidized arms sales.
4. A defense treaty with the United States operationalized as a dummy variable.
5. The gross size of imports to the recipient state, from the Union of Soviet Socialist Republics.
6. The gross size of exports from the recipient state to the Union of Soviet Socialist Republics.
7. Imports to the Union of Soviet Socialist Republics as a total percentage of recipient state exports.

8. Exports from the recipient state to Union of Soviet as a percentage of total recipient state exports
9. The gross level of communist economic aid from all communist block sources.
10. An index of Union of Soviet Socialist Republics security ties consisting of the presence or absence of Union of Soviet Socialist Republics' military aid, arm transfers, defense treaties, military bases, military technicians, or military advisors, standardized and indexed. The presence of each tie is assigned the value "1" the absence the value "0". The values are then added and divided by "6", the number of ties being measured.

The index to measure the Union of Soviet Socialist Republics security ties was necessary because of the lack of reliable and consistent annual data concerning the gross level of Union of Soviet Socialist Republics military aid and arm transfers to recipient states. However, the inclusion of gross measures for the United States and indexed measures for the U.S.S.R. may bias the model.

To avoid this potential, a second security model is operationalized that replaces the indicators for United States military aid, arm transfers, defense treaty and bases with an index identical to the Union of Soviet Socialist

Republics security index. The advantage of the second security model is the decrease in the number of independent variables and a more comparable measure of the relative security relations between the recipient state and the United States and U.S.S.R. However, the disadvantage of the second security model is the loss of sensitivity in relation to the impact of specific security related decision making determinants.

THE GEOPOLITICAL MODEL

The geopolitical model is operationalized with seven indicators designed to measure the power capabilities or potential of the recipient state. The model closely replicates McKinlay and Little's research.

1. The gross population of the recipient state.
2. The gross domestic product of the recipient state, adjusted to avoid simultaneous causation. (GDP - Level of A.I.D. economic assistance)
3. Recipient state gross international reserves.
4. Recipient state gross military expenditures.
5. Recipient state military expenditures as a percent of total GNP.
6. The size of the recipient state's military establishment in thousands of members.

7. The size of the recipient state's military establishment as the number of members per thousands of population.

THE ECONOMIC SELF INTEREST MODEL

The economic self interest model is operationalized with six indicators that closely replicate McKinlay and Little's model and are designed to measure the economic relationship between the United States and the recipient state.

1. The gross size of United States imports to the recipient state.
2. The gross size of exports from the recipient state to the United States.
3. United States imports to the recipient state as a percent of total imports.
4. Exports from the recipient state to the United States as a percentage of total exports.
5. The balance between foreign investment in the recipient state by nonresidents and the level of investment by recipient state residents outside the recipient state. (Investment by nonresidents - Investment outside recipient state by residents)
6. Net total investment in the recipient state from all sources foreign and domestic.

Research Design

THE DEVELOPMENT INTEREST MODEL

The development interest model is operationalized with six indicators that measure the size and rate of economic growth, the level of domestic investment, and the level of economic activity for specific sectors of the economy. The model replicates McKinlay and Little's research with the addition of a measure for the size of the agriculture sector of the recipient state's economy.

1. Adjusted gross domestic product.
2. The percent of gross domestic product in manufacturing economic activities.
3. The percentage of gross domestic product in mining economic activities.
4. The percentage of gross domestic product in agricultural economic activities.
5. The annual change in gross domestic product.
6. Total gross domestic investment from resident sources.

THE POLITICAL IDEOLOGY MODEL

As noted McKinlay and Little's political stability and democracy model failed to adequately capture both phenomenon. To measure the political ideology of the recipient state, McKinlay and Little's indicators are replaced with the measures and index developed by Kenneth Bollen. Bollen's index of political democracy consists of two sets of indicators designed to measure popular sovereignty and political liberties. (Bollen:83:75)

Subsequent research and application of Bollen's measure of political democracy by Bollen and Jackman have found the index to be both reliable and consistent. (Bollen and Jackman:85/Bollen and Jackman:85) However, Bollen's research, and subsequent research, on the measurement of political democracy does not provide an index for all recipient states of the data set for the temporal period. Consequently, it is necessary to replicate Bollen's measures or to locate a data source providing the necessary measures for the recipient states of the data set throughout the temporal period.

Replication of Bollen's index for over seventy recipient states for a nine year period represents a substantial research project in and of itself. Consequently, it was decided to adopt the index of political liberties and civil rights available through the "World Handbook of Social and Political Indicators III". Unfortunately, the "The World Handbook III" provides its indexes for only four years of the temporal period, 1973-1976.

Research Design

Being unwilling to limit the analysis of the political ideology model for the last four years of the temporal period, and intensive search was conducted to locate a second data source that contained the necessary indexes. Unfortunately, no alternative data source could be located. After due consideration, it was decided to operationalize a second political ideology model, based on the annual events data of the "World Handbook of Social and Political Indicators III".

The second political ideology model breaks Bollen's index into its component parts, but does not develop a comparable index to measure the relative level of democratic development. The events data operationalized for the second political ideology model indicate whether the government of the recipient state has taken action which is consistent or inconsistent with the continuation or expansion of popular sovereignty and political liberties. Consequently, the second political ideology model is testing a variant of the political ideology hypothesis presented.

The political ideology hypothesis predicts that the level of bilateral foreign aid allocated to recipient states is partly determined by the recipient state's level of democratic development. This hypothesis will be tested for the years 1973-1976 by the first political ideology model.

Research Design

The second political ideology model tests whether specific events, such as elections, that are perceived as enhancing or detrimental to the development of political democracy affect the allocation of bilateral foreign aid.

The rationale behind the second political ideology model is that if an event occurring in the recipient state is perceived on the part of the Executive or Congressional decision makers as movement towards the development of political democracy, then the decision makers will respond by increasing the level of foreign aid. Conversely, if events are perceived as movement away from the development of political democracy, the level of foreign aid will be adversely affected.

While the second political ideology model does not measure the level of democratic development, it has one advantage to the first ideology model. It is likely that the allocation of bilateral aid is effected by certain events, such as elections. However, the occurrence of an election will not necessarily cause a change of Bollen's measure of political democracy.

If the state in question is already classified as being democratic then the occurrence of an election will have no impact on the measure of democratic development. Whether decision makers respond to the level of democratic development, or respond to specific events, can be determined by regressing both models against the dependent variables and comparing the results.

The first political ideology model is operationalized with two indicators designed to replicate Bollen's measures of popular sovereignty and political liberties.

1. Political Rights index, with a score of 1 indicating a high degree of political rights and a score of 7 indicating a low level of political rights.
2. Civil Rights index, with a score of 1 indicating a high level of civil liberties, and a score of 7 indicating a low level of civil rights.

The second political ideology model is operationalized with four event indicators, derived from the component parts of Bollen's measure of political democracy, that record events that are either consistent or inconsistent with development of political democracy. However, this model is more successful in recording events related to political liberties than events related to popular sovereignty.

1. The occurrence of an election for chief Executive, national assembly, or policy referendum at the

national level. Excluded are elections by national assemblies, party Congresses, trade union councils, or political parties. There are no exclusions for suffrage limitations, competitiveness, or other indicators of the fairness of the election.

2. Imposition of domestic political sanctions including the imposition of censorship on newspapers, magazines, books, radio, or television, and actions taken by the recipient state to neutralize or suppress or eliminate political opposition.
3. Relaxation of domestic political sanctions including the modification or elimination of controls on mass media and other sanctions designed to limit the political powers of the polity.
4. Freedom of group opposition measured as the occurrence of protest demonstration and other forms of group dissent or protest against the regime.

THE POLITICAL STABILITY MODEL

McKinlay and Little combine political stability and democracy into one model. However, as noted in Chapter Three, there is substantial evidence to suggest that the two phenomenon are distinct and require independent measurement. To operationalize the political stability model, seven indicators, developed by Daniel Geller, are adopted.

Research Design

1. The occurrence of political strikes on the part of industrial or service workers, or the stoppage of academic activity by students as a protest against the regime, its policy or actions.
2. The occurrence of riots that include the presence of violence on the part of the protesters or police.
3. The occurrence of protest demonstrations; this is the sole indicator in common between the political ideology and political security models.
4. The occurrence of political assassination defined as a politically motivated murder of a high ranking government official, at the national or local level, including prominent politicians not currently holding office.
5. Armed attacks carried out by organized groups against the regime, or by the armed forces of the regime against organized groups perceived as insurgents or as a serious security threat to the regime.
6. The occurrence of an unsuccessful attempt by persons not holding national Executive office to legally obtain such office.

7. The occurrence of an irregular transfer of Executive power from one person or group outside the legal or customary procedures for the transfer of Executive power.

THE DOMESTIC INTEREST MODEL

The domestic interest model operationalizes six indicators designed to measure the strength of the donor state's economy and domestic political pressures. The model tests both the domestic economic interest and the reelection hypotheses. Each of the indicators is regressed independently against the dependent variables for methodological reasons.

1. The level of donor state unemployment.
2. The change in the donor state's GNP from the previous year.
3. The total economic aid budget as a percentage of the total donor state budget, to measure the impact of available foreign aid funds on the allocation of A.I.D. economic aid across recipient states.
4. The level of multilateral aid including loans and grants from all sources.

5. The gross aggregate value of United States farm crops, excluding the value of meat and meat by-products.
6. Presidential, or Congressional election year.

TABLE THREE

A COMPARISON OF ONE AND TWO YEAR INFORMATION LAG AS MEASURED BY R SQUARED

	GENERAL	MILITARY	ECONOMIC
ONE YEAR	78%	49%	77%
TWO YEAR	67%	85%	71%

(Kato:69:204)

FIGURE TEN

THE ANALYTIC SCHEME

INDEPENDENT VARIABLES ORGANIZATIONAL GOALS:	DEPENDENT VARIABLES DECISION OUTCOMES:
GOOD POLICY GOALS:	
donor security interest	Executive Branch
donor geopolitical interest	budgetary request
donor economic self interest	
developmental interest	
political ideology interest	
systemic stability interest	Congressional
recipient needs	appropriations
donor domestic economy	
INSTITUTIONAL GOALS:	
influence over foreign aid policy goal	
member reelection goal	

CHAPTER FIVE

EMPIRICAL RESULTS AND CONCLUSIONS

"Recipient Need Model: There is no support for the hypothesis derived from the recipient need model." "Donor Interest Model: The findings for all the years provide strong confirmation for the donor interest model." (McKinlay and Little:79:243)

"We therefore conclude that if an appropriate model is used it is not possible, contrary to the contention of Mckinlay and Little, to reject the hypothesis that recipient need is a significant determinant of the pattern of aid allocation for most Western capitalist countries." (Mosley:81:253)

"The major deviations from the predictions include: (a) high saliency of domestic economy in nonstrategic military aid allocation and the lack of saliency in nonstrategic economic aid"

(Kato:69:210)

As noted in Chapter Four, the models were tested for heteroscedasticity and auto-correlation. The test for heteroscedasticity were all negative, consequently, no corrective action was taken and it is assumed that the variance of the error term across cases is constant.

The Durbin-Watson test statistic for auto-correlation indicated that the domestic models are not negatively auto-correlated. For the sample size and for the number of explanatory variables, the null hypotheses that the models contain no positive auto-correlation is accepted for the proportion of total United States budget, multilateral, and unemployment indicators. The indicators for farm prices and change in donor state GNP fall between the upper and lower limits of the test statistic, and the results are indeterminate. The economic aid as a percent of total budget, and reelection indicators were found to be positively auto-correlated. For these indicators there will be a tendency to reject the null hypothesis when it should be accepted.

In addition to the hypotheses operationalized, several secondary propositions have been put forth. Only two of the secondary were statistically tested; 1) whether the 1973 Basic Human Needs amendments represent a fourth foreign aid period, and 2) whether the differences in legal authorizations and administrative structure across foreign aid programs cause independent allocation patterns. The remaining secondary questions are matters for future investigation.

The coefficient of determination, or the R squared statistic, will be used to determine the transitive relationship between the explanatory models. However, as noted by King, there are limitations to the use of R squared. The R squared statistic is a useful measure for cross model analysis when comparing "two equations with different explanatory variables and identical dependent variables." (King:86:677)

Consequently, R squared is an appropriate statistic to independently determine the foreign aid preferences for the Executive and Congress; but is inappropriate for comparison across the dependent variables. To compare the explanatory power of equations with different dependent variables, and to define the strength and direction of the causal relationship, it is necessary to consider the unstandardized regression coefficient.

The significance of several independent variables was limited to one year. These cases are probably caused by unique events in the recipient, or donor state. For example, the Military expenditures as a percent of GNP indicator was found to have a significant association with

Congressional appropriations for one year, 1969. (see Table Seven) The positive relationship is probably the result of unusually large arm purchases by certain recipient states, or could be caused by events in Southeast Asia.

Such cases may indicate a level of sensitivity, on the part of foreign aid decision makers, to international, or bilateral events. As such the unique events that cause the relationship may be of interest as case studies. However, the concern here is to identify the foreign aid decision making determinants that cause the annual, or routine allocation of economic assistance. Generally the unique cases do not contribute to our understanding of the general allocation pattern, unless the case illustrates a changing or emerging distribution pattern. For example, the significance of several predictor variables was limited to fiscal year 1976. Indicating that 1976 may mark a change in foreign aid policy. However, while such cases are of interest, consideration is limited because they tend to be isolated events.

DISCUSSION OF THE EXPLANATORY MODELS

To determine whether the foreign aid decision making determinants vary significantly between the Executive and Legislative branches of government, it is first necessary to determine the relationship between the requests for foreign aid funds and appropriations. To test the significance of this relationship, the Executive request for funds was regressed against Congressional appropriations; the relationship was positive and significant for all years.

It was found that the Executive has a significant affect on Congressional foreign aid decisions. However, the explanatory power of the independent variable, the Executive request for funds, as measured by the unstandardized regression coefficient, and R squared, varied over the study period. An indication that the relationship is unstable, in that it varies significantly from year to year.
(see Table Five)

The examination of the unstandardized coefficient indicates that Congress routinely cuts the Executive request for funds. (see Table Five) The value of the unstandardized coefficients was less than one, indicating that for every one dollar requested by the Executive (the independent variable), the actual level appropriated by Congress (the dependent variable) was less than one dollar. (See Table Five) This conclusion is supported by comparing the means of the independent and dependent variable by year. The Congress cut foreign aid budgetary requests by an average of forty-one percent (41%) over the temporal period, however, the level of cuts varied substantially; from a low of 14% for fiscal year 1970 to a high of 50% for fiscal year 1975. (See Table Six)

The significances, and direction, of the relationship supports the proposition that Congressional appropriations are a response to the Executive request for funds. The foreign aid agenda is set by the Executive. However, the size of the unexplained variance, and the differences in the relationship over time, is an indication that Congress significantly alters the Executive's request for aid. This is a necessary condition, but not sufficient, to accept the proposition that the decision making determinants vary significantly between the two institutions. Whether to reject or accept the null hypothesis is dependent upon the analysis of the explanatory models.

Of the nine models tested, only the first political ideology model failed to show a significant relationship throughout the temporal period, for both dependent variables. The first political ideology model adopts Bollen's index of political democracy. Based on this analysis there is no support for the proposition that the United States allocates bilateral economic aid based on the recipient state's level of democratic development. The explanatory power of the remaining models varied over time, but each was found to be significant for at least one year.

The rank order of the eight models that tested positive for at least one year was independently determined for the Executive and Congress using the R squared statistic. For both branches, the three most significant foreign aid strategies included; the geopolitical power model, recipient need model, and the political stability model, respectfully. While the rank order for the first three models was identical for both branches, there are significant differences between institutions. Suggesting, that while there is a level of decision making consistency across institutions, there remain important differences.

As was the case with McKinlay and Little's research, the most salient explanatory model was the geopolitical. There is strong support for the hypothesis that the United States allocates economic aid on the basis of the power potential of the recipient state. The most prominent decision making determinants for the geopolitical model, in order are; 1) the size of the military per 1000 population, 2) international reserves, and 3) population. The remaining two indicators are valid for one or two fiscal years. (see Table Seven)

Conclusions

The most significant decision making determinant was the level of the recipient state's militarism, as measured by size of the military per 1000 population. (see Table Seven) For the Executive request, the indicator was salient throughout the study period. The same was not true for appropriations, where the geopolitical model was not significant for 1970 and 1975. An indication that while both institutions tend to allocate economic aid based on the geopolitical power potential of the recipient state, there are disagreements across institutions and over time concerning the emphasis placed on each decision making determinant.

In general the findings concerning militarism support McKinlay and Little's research. While there are important differences in research design between McKinlay and Little's research and this project, it is nevertheless clear that the level of potential geopolitical power has been a significant consideration in the allocation of economic assistance from 1960 through 1976. While the strength of the relationship has varied over the sixteen year period, the findings indicate that the level of geopolitical power, particularly the level of militarism, is an important and enduring foreign aid decision making determinant.

Conclusions

One significant difference between the policy priorities of the Congress and the Executive is captured by the international reserves measure. The Executive considers the level of international reserves held by the recipient state an important determinant for the allocation of foreign aid. The relationship between international reserves and the Executive's request for foreign aid is significant for all years. However, Congress does not share the Executive's perspective and the validity of the indicator is limited to 1976. The Executives emphasis on the level of international reserves is probably an illustration of the influence of the Treasury Department on the Executive decision making process. (see Chapter Three) The Congress apparently does not share Treasury's concern.

While the population indicator showed a significant relationship with both the Congress and the Executive, the level of association tended to be rather weak; the highest R squared score was .09. (see Table Seven) While the level of association is rather weak, population is a traditional measure of a states power potential, and the saliency of the indicator is considered additional support for the geopolitical hypothesis.

The recipient need model was significant through out the temporal period. However, the human condition indicators were generally not significant. Life expectancy and infant mortality were both significant for one year; but there is no evidence that the relationship indicates a new or emerging allocation pattern resulting from the 1973 basic human needs amendments. The human condition of the recipient state has no substantive impact on the foreign aid decision making process. These findings are consistent with Mosley's conclusions that "life expectancy, the literacy rate . . . had no significant influence at any point." (Mosley:81:248)

In contrast to the human condition measures, two of the economic need measures, the balance of payments, and the per capita indicators, were significant and positive for both institutions. (see Table Eight) The positive relationship with the per capita GNP measure means that as the level of per capita GNP increases the level of aid increases. To support the recipient need hypothesis a negative relationship is necessary; the positive relationship falsifies the recipient need hypothesis. Also, if one assumes that the level of per capita GNP is a rough estimate of a states economic power, the positive relationship tends to support the hypothesis that foreign aid is allocated based on the recipients potential economic power in addition to geopolitical power.

Conclusions

The positive relationship with the balance of payments measure means that as the recipient state's of balance of payments increase, or as the balance of payments situation deteriorates, the level of aid increases. This positive association is interpreted as supporting the hypothesis that the donor considers the economic needs of the recipient state in the decision making process. The empirical results for the balance of payments and per capita GNP measures tend to be more significant than Mosley's. (Mosley:81:248)

While the empirical results concerning the human condition measure are rather clear, the results of the economic measures are mixed. The per capita measure tends to falsify the recipient need hypothesis, while the balance of payments measure supports the hypothesis. However, starting in 1975, the analysis shows a change in foreign aid distribution pattern that may indicate a change in policy. For the recipient need model, the allocation of foreign aid began changing in 1975, and by the 1976 fiscal year, the allocation pattern was found to be unique from previous years. For the 1976 fiscal year, per capita GNP was not significant for both institutions, while the balance of payments indicator was significant and positive. (see Table Eight)

Conclusions

The uniqueness of the 1976 allocation pattern may be the result of policy differences between President Ford and President Nixon, or it might be caused by the 1973 oil embargo and corresponding oil price increases. However, the new pattern may also illustrate the emerging impact of the 1973 human condition amendments. The question is whether the recipient need hypothesis should be rejected or conditionally accepted? The human needs portion of the hypothesis is rejected: but the hypothesis that assistance is allocated based partly on the economic needs of the recipient state can not be accepted or rejected with confidence.

One final note, concerning the recipient need model, is that the research design and explanatory model operationalized are based on previous research in the field. The theoretical foundations of the approach include the assumption that a humanitarian, or recipient need, based foreign aid policy, can be identified by measuring the allocation pattern across recipient states. There is, however, a competing conceptualization noted in Chapter Two.

It is feasible that a humanitarian policy is reflected by an intrastate, rather than an interstate foreign aid allocations. The intrastate criteria raises the question of which segment of the population within the recipient state, is targeted by the foreign aid policy of the donor state. The advantage of this approach is the recognition that the basic human needs of some segment of the population go unmet, for each recipient.

Still, the overall, or general, allocation pattern across recipient states, found by this and other research, suggest that foreign aid is primarily a tool of foreign policy allocated to reflect the various interest of the donor state. Consequently, other than disaster aid, which was omitted from the measure of aid operationalized for this analysis, any humanitarian policy is pursued within the context of the donors self interest.

For the Executive, the stability model was significant for five years, 1970, and 1972 through 1975. (see Table Nine) Generally the Congressional model was less powerful than the Executive model, but in 1969 and 1974 the relationship was reversed. McKinlay and Little misspecified the stability model, thus is no basis for comparison.

The significance of the model for both dependent variables is almost exclusively the result of a positive relationship with the armed attack measure. The other indicators do not appear to have a substantive or consistent impact on the allocation of foreign aid. The value of the unstandardized coefficient for the armed attacked indicator, however, varies significantly between institutions, and from one year to the next. (see Table Nine) Indicating an unstable and varying relationship over time and between the two institutions.

Despite significant variances between the Executive request and Congressional appropriations, the simple rank order of the three explanatory models considered is the same for both institutions, in that the geopolitical model had the greatest explanatory power for both institutions, followed by the recipient needs and stability models respectfully. At this point, however, the relative import of the explanatory models varies across the domestic institutions. The consideration of the empirical models will continue based on the findings for the Executive.

The fourth most powerful foreign aid strategy for the Executive is the second political ideology model which was significant for three years; 1968, 1970 and 1974. However, the relationship is not caused by any particular decision making determinant. All indicators are salient for at least one year with no indicator being significant for more than three years. The most salient determinant, for the Executive, is the protest demonstrations indicator, but the relationship is unstable in that the sign of the unstandardized coefficient is inconsistent; switching from negative for 1970 to positive for 1972 and 1975.

For the Congress the findings are equally mixed. The most salient indicator is the occurrence of elections in the recipient state. The relationship is positive for 1968 and 1969, indicating that if the recipient state held an election in the year prior to appropriations the level of aid tended to increase. By 1974, however, the relationship reversed itself, and holding elections tended to decrease the level of foreign aid.

For the Executive the remaining four models derived from the international approach, the economic self interest, developmental interest, and the two security models had very limited explanatory power. Each of these models showed a significant relationship for one year of the temporal period. (see Table Eleven - Sixteen) It does not appear that these foreign aid decision making strategies play a substantive role in the Executive's request for bilateral economic foreign aid. For the economic self interest and development interest models, these findings are consistent with the Congressional models and with McKinlay and Little's research.

Conclusions

For the Executive request, both R squared and the unstandardized coefficient indicate that the security interests of the donor state is a minor consideration. The findings for the Congressional models, however, rank the security interests of the donor state as the fourth most important decision making determinant with substantially greater explanatory power than the developmental, domestic, or economic self interest models. (see Tables Eleven and Twelve)

In contrast to these results, McKinlay and Little ranked the security interests of the donor state as the second most significant explanation for the allocation of bilateral foreign aid. However, it must be remembered that the research design is limited to economic assistance while McKinlay and Little combined military and economic aid.

The significant relationship between appropriations and the security interest of the donor state was unanticipated. Based on the review of the domestic literature, it was thought, given the strong Congressional reaction to the Vietnam War and the basic Human Needs amendments of 1973, that the Executive branch would request funds to reflect United States security interests, but the Congress would alter these allocation patterns and decrease the saliency of the security models. The statistical analysis does not support these conclusions.

A second unanticipated relationship was between the Food for Peace Program and the security models. The first security model was the most successful in explaining Food for Peace allocations. (see Tables Eleven and Seventeen) The findings concerning the allocations for the Food for Peace program support the hypothesis that the varying legal authorizations and institutional relationships across foreign aid programs causes unique allocation patterns. The relationship between Food for Peace allocations and the security models also provides important insights into United States foreign aid policy.

There is no support in this analysis for the hypothesis that the allocation of United States bilateral economic aid is affected by changes in the domestic economy of the donor state. The foreign aid budget, over the temporal period, has tended to decrease, however, this decrease is not apparently caused by fluctuations in the domestic economy. Nor is there any evidence that the allocation of A.I.D. administered aid is effected by the level of domestic farm prices. (see Table Thirteen)

Conclusions

There is no support for Pastor's hypothesis that the 1973 basic human needs amendments caused a change in the allocation of United States bilateral economic aid. The acceptance or rejection of the proposition depends primarily on the validity of the human condition measures operationalized to test the recipient need model. To accept Pastor's hypothesis, it is necessary that the change in allocation pattern reflect the relative human needs of the recipient state.

The recipient need model was not accepted or rejected for two reasons; 1) the change in the allocation pattern for fiscal year 1976 and, 2) because of the positive relationship with the balance of payments indicator. However, there is no evidence that the 1976 allocation pattern reflects the basic human condition of the recipient state. Any impact of the 1973 amendments apparently reflects the economic needs of the recipient state rather than human needs. Consequently, the fourth foreign aid period, hypothesized by Pastor, is rejected.

There is limited support for the hypothesis that, for the Executive, the occurrence of a domestic election causes a change in the allocation of economic foreign aid. (see Table Thirteen) The relationship is positive and slightly greatly than one. Indicating that during election years the

Executive tends to request higher levels of foreign aid than during nonelection years. However, the model was found to be positively auto-correlated, consequently the relationship maybe stronger than indicated. (see Table Fifteen)

The hypothesis that the variance in legal authorizations and formal policy criteria causes an unique allocation pattern for each foreign aid program is accepted. According to this proposition the donor state has a set of policy objectives that can be pursued through the allocation of foreign aid. To pursue these goals the donor state develops a series of specialized programs each designed to achieve or pursue varying policy alternatives.

The hypothesis is derived from Kato's conclusions that the allocation of military aid varied significantly from the allocation of economic aid. (see Chapter Two) For this study, the level of military aid was operationalized as an independent variable in the first security model, and there was no relationship with either dependent variable. (see Chapter Four, and Table Eleven)

Additional support is found in a comparison between this research and McKinlay and Little's findings. There are several similarities, but there are also important differences. For example, McKinlay and Little found the security interest of the donor state to be the second most important foreign aid strategy. The same was model ranked fourth for Congressional appropriations, and was found not to be an important consideration for the Executive in this analysis. It is hypothesized that the differences in research findings are caused by the differences in the dependent variable. (see Tables Seven through Seventeen, and Table One)

To further test this hypothesis, Food for Peace appropriations were operationalized as a dependent variable and tested against the explanatory models. There is no intent to provide an intensive review of the Food for Peace Program, and it should be noted that the data set utilized is based on the recipients of United States bilateral economic aid administered by Agency for International Development. Recipients receiving military or Food for Peace assistance, but not Agency for International Development administered economic aid, are excluded. Consequently, the data set is not adequate to make an exhaustive or determinative comparison of foreign aid programs.

However, given these limitations it is clear that the allocation pattern reported for the Food for Peace program varies significantly from the Congressional appropriations for Agency for International Development and from the total aid allocations reported by McKinlay and Little. (see Tables Seven through Seventeen)

Important differences were also noted for the domestic model. A weak but significant relationship was found between the allocation of Food for Peace funds and three domestic indicators; economic aid as a percentage of the total United States budget, the allocation of multilateral aid, and domestic farm prices. (see Table Fifteen) The relationship with the United States budget and multilateral aid is positive. Unlike economic aid there appears to be some coordination between bilateral food aid and the distribution of aid by international agencies.

The positive relationship with the budget indicator means that when the non-military foreign aid budget is increased, the Food for Peace budget will also increase. The lack of relationship between A.I.D.'s budget and the United States budget measure implies that the Food for Peace budget will be increased before A.I.D.'s budget is increased. It appears that the budget for the Food for Peace program is expanded to either achieve foreign policy goals that can not be achieved with A.I.D. programs, or the program's budget is increased for reasons other than foreign policy. This may be evidence that the Food for Peace program has more domestic political support that economic assistance administered by A.I.D..

The negative relationship with the farm price indicator means that when the value of domestic crops decreases, which presumably implies a large surplus, the level of Food for Peace allocations increases. Suggesting that the Food for Peace program has a level of domestic support that is adequate to influence budget allocations. This relationship, when combined with the positive relationship between total economic foreign aid budget and the Food for Peace budget, supports Ripley and Franklin's observation that the Food for Peace Program is unique among foreign aid programs because of significant political support from agricultural interests. (Ripley and Franklin:84:242-243) (See Chapter Three)

CONCLUSIONS

The statistical analysis revealed a significant correlation between several of the independent variables and the allocation of foreign aid; but few of the independent variables are reliable predictors. To reliably predict the allocation of foreign aid, a variable must demonstrate a significant and consistent relationship over time. Most of the significant relationships identified were of limited duration, or the indicator showed both a positive and negative relationship over time.

Of the thirty-one indicators found to be significant for at least one observation, only four are considered both consistent and reliable; 1) the size of recipient state's military per thousand population, 2) the level of the recipient state's international reserves, 3) per capita GNP and, 4) the number of armed attacks against the recipient state. Each of these indicators showed a significant and consistent relationship for at least five years. The four indicators are from the three most powerful models, the geopolitical, recipient need, and the stability model.

The preeminence of these four indicator raises two methodological questions. The first is whether they are independent of each other. This is particularity a concern for the size of the military per thousands, the number of armed attacks and the per capita GNP indicators. It is reasonable to suspect that recipient state's with the highest per capita GNP can also afford the largest military. It is also reasonable to suspect that there is a relationship between the number of armed attacks and the size of the recipients military, particularity when one considers the high level of foreign aid and the chronic instability of the Indo-China region during the temporal period.

The second methodological question is concerned with a the potential for multicolinearity between the independent variables of the original models. The explanatory power of the original models is largely derived from the four indicators noted. With one exception, the other significant independent variables of the original models are valid for one to three years. The exception is the size of military per thousand and the international reserves indicators. Both are derived from the geopolitical model, and, for the Executive, both are significant for five or more years.

To test for the independence of the four indicators, a composite model was operationalized and regressed against the Executives request for foreign aid funds, and Congressional appropriations. (see Table Sixteen) All four indicators were found to be significant, however the value of R squared and the unstandardized regression coefficient varied between the composite model and the original models. In general, the number of significant observations decreased for the per capita and armed attacks indicators. The findings for the size of military and international reserves were more consistent with the results of the original analysis. (see Tables Sixteen, Seven, Eight, and Nine)

Conclusions

The statistical analysis indicates some level of interaction between the per capita, armed attacks and the size of the recipients military indicators. Still given that these predictor variables were significant for both the original and composite models, it is reasonable to assume a substantial level of independence. However, the per capita and armed attacks indicators should be considered secondary decision making determinants.

Based on these findings, it is assumed that for both the Executive and Congress the size of the recipients military is the primary decision making determinant. Of nearly equal importance, to the Executive, is the level of the recipient state's international reserves. The Congress strongly disagrees with the Executive, however, and does not consider the international reserves determinant when deciding how much foreign aid to allocate to which recipient.

It is interesting to note that the explanatory power of the per capita measure, for both the combined and original models, is generally greater for the Executive than for Congress. When combined with the international reserves measure, this may be an indication that the Executive has adopted an economic-political power strategy to supplement its geopolitical power strategy. Unfortunately an economic political power model was not operationalized, nor has the necessary theoretical foundations been established. Still, given the significance of the two indicators, and the failure of the economic self interest model, it is quite possible that the Executive has adopted a foreign aid strategy designed to improve bilateral relations with recipients that have a significant economic potential, regardless of the economic interests of the donor state.

Based on the unstandardized regression coefficients, of both the original and composite models, the primary hypothesis that there are significant differences in the foreign aid policy preferences between the Executive and Congress is accepted. The strongest disagreements in policy priorities were found in the security models, and for the international reserves indicator. However, while these differences are adequate to accept the hypothesis, the results also indicate that the Executive dominates the formation of foreign aid policy.

Ripley and Franklin classify all forms of foreign aid, except for the Food for Peace Program, as strategic international policy. As strategic policy, foreign aid is dominated by the Executive branch. However, if Congress becomes actively involved in the decision making process conflict over policy alternatives will occur, resulting in compromise. (Ripley & Franklin:84:100-102,243,228-229) The conflict over policy alternatives has been aptly described in the domestic literature, and the empirical results indicate that the observable allocation of foreign aid is the result of compromise between the Executive and Congress.

The allocation of United States bilateral economic foreign aid administered by Agency for International Development, therefore, is the result of an intensive debate, over policy priorities, between the Executive and Congress. Since neither branch has the legal-constitutional authority to independently determine foreign aid policy, foreign aid decisions and the resulting pattern of foreign aid allocations, is the result of a compromise between institutions.

As strategic policy, the Executive remains the dominant branch and the most important influence in the determination of policy. Based on the empirical results of this analysis, Ripley and Franklin's classification of foreign aid as strategic policy is accepted, and future research on the allocation of foreign aid should be guided by this classification. (Ripley & Franklin:84:100-102,243, 228-229)

The empirical analysis also confirms McKinlay and Little conclusions that the allocation of foreign aid is largely determined by the self interest of the donor state.

(McKinlay and Little:79:243) Consequently, economic foreign aid is correctly classified as an instrument of foreign policy. The significant models and independent variables suggest that the United States has adopted a systemic foreign aid policy. The basic premise of a systemic policy is to allocate foreign aid to maintain the donor state's position within the international system. To achieve this goal the donor state adopts foreign aid strategies designed to; 1) promote systemic stability, when such stability is in the donor's interest, 2) to acquire allies, and 3) to limit the influence of competing states.

The stability strategy is best illustrated by the validity of the stability model. This suggests that the United States allocates increased aid to recipients suffering from armed attacked. Since the states in question are already receiving economic aid, it can be is assumed that the maintenance of the current regime is usually in the systemic interest of the United States.

The acquisition of allies strategy is supported by the geopolitical model. Also the positive findings for the per capita GNP measure adds support to the proposition that the donor state allocates foreign aid to secure allies among the stronger third world states.

Conclusions

The final strategy of the systemic foreign policy goal, to limit the influence of competing states, is more complex in that the strategy can be broken into two subcategories; the leverage and containment strategies. The leverage strategy predicts that the United States will allocate economic aid to recipient states with communist block relations in order to maintain some minimum level of influence, or leverage, over the foreign and domestic policy of recipient state. The containment strategy predicts that aid will be allocated to reward recipients with security ties and to penalize recipients with communist sympathies.

The indicators measuring bilateral security ties were operationalized to test the security model. In general, the empirical findings for the security model support the containment strategy, but the overall explanatory power is limited and, other than the absence of a relationship, there is little support for the leverage strategy. However, it is reasonable to assume that the United States would not utilize the same foreign aid program to implement both the leverage and containment strategies.

The rationale behind this proposition is quite simple. Military aid has the potential of increasing the military capacity of a potentially hostile state. Consequently, military aid is allocated to reflects a containment strategy, but not a leverage strategy. Economic aid has the potential of assisting in the development of a centrally planned economy which is not in the United States security or economic interests. Based on the results obtained here, it appears that economic assistance is used primarily in the acquisition of allies and the promotion of systemic stability.

In contrast food aid is less likely to increase the economic or military capacity of a recipient state with ties to the communist block, while allowing the United States to maintain its leverage. Of all the forms of aid, the U.S.S.R. is least capable of providing food aid. Which has the effect of increasing the United States leverage in relation to the U.S.S.R., since the cancellation of Food For Peace aid cannot be easily replaced by food aid by the U.S.S.R.. Given this rationale, one might expect, Food for Peace allocations to be more strongly related to recipient states with communist block ties than economic aid administered by A.I.D.. The findings support this proposition. (see Table Eleven and Twelve) In particular, only Food for Peace allocations are positively related to the U.S.S.R. security interest index.

The classification of foreign economic aid as strategic foreign policy supports the realist perspective of the international system. While there is evidence that the United States has developed specific foreign aid programs to achieve varying foreign policy goals, it does not appear that these goals include altruistic or humanitarian objectives. In consideration of this conclusion please note that, by intent, the research design adopted reflects a best case scenario for the recipient need model.

If the United States allocated aid to reflect human need, it would most likely take the form of economic or food aid. The two primary programs to allocate food and economic aid were operationalized and independently tested in this analysis. And, while the analysis for the Food for Peace Program is incomplete, it appears clear that allocation of both economic and food aid reflect the systemic interests of the donor state and not the basic human needs of the recipient state.

Like all research the conclusion here are limited by the research design and methodology adopted. It is possible that the recipient need model has been misspecified, or missmeasured, or that the 1973 basic human needs amendments began to effect foreign aid policy after 1976; further research concerning the recipient need model is necessary. Such research should consider additional or alternative theoretical conceptualizations, such as the intrastate allocation question noted. However, one must be careful not to confuse the form of foreign aid with the context of its allocation. Most of the aid administered by the Agency for International Development, the Food for Peace program, and the Peace Corps is humanitarian in its form. But, the evidence from this and earlier research suggest that the allocation of bilateral foreign aid by the United States, is within the context of the donor state's self interest.

TABLE FOUR

A COMPARISON OF R SQUARED FOR THE GROSS AND PER CAPITA MEASURES FOR THE RECIPIENT NEEDS AND GEOPOLITICAL MODELS

PART ONE
RECIPIENT NEEDS MODEL

	YEAR								
MEASURES	68	69	70	71	72	73	74	75	76
REQUEST	XX	90	92	XX	91	87	92	90	32
REQUEST PERCAPITA	XX	45	60	XX	43	40	42	50	27
APPROP.	88	88	25	92	83	70	93	36	NS
APPROP. PERCAPITA	37	38	23	61	39	34	56	NS	36

NS = not significant
XX = data not available

TABLE FOUR

PART TWO
GEOPOLITICAL POWER MODEL

MEASURES	YEAR 68	69	70	71	72	73	74	75	76
REQUEST	XX	76	79	XX	68	68	70	73	88
REQUEST PERCAPITA	XX	51	56	XX	50	64	65	75	53
APPROP.	70	74	NS	80	68	54	71	69	40
APPROP. PERCAPITA	39	56	NS	55	48	54	60	NS	44

NS
= not significant
XX = data not available

TABLE FIVE

THE VARIANCE BETWEEN THE EXECUTIVE REQUEST AND CONGRESSIONAL APPROPRIATIONS FOR A.I.D. FUNDS

MEASURES	YEAR 68	69	70	71	72	73	74	75	76
R SQUARED	XX	49	28	XX	60	31	55	27	55
UNSTANDARDIZED COEEFFICIENT*	XX	47	69	XX	56	33	55	23	47

*all values are positive

TABLE SIX

A COMPARISON BETWEEN THE MEAN A.I.D. FOREIGN AID ALLOCATION FOR THE EXECUTIVE REQUEST AND CONGRESSIONAL APPROPRIATIONS

	YEAR								
MEASURES	68	69	70	71	72	73	74	75	76
REQUEST	XX	3.7*	2.7	XX	4.2	4.2	3.3	4.5	2.7
APPROP.	2.4	1.8	2.5	2.0	2.0	1.8	1.8	1.9	1.6
% DIFF.	XX	.51	.14	XX	.52	.57	.45	.58	.41

MEAN FIGURES FOR PERIOD: REQUEST = 3.4
APPROP. = 2.0
DIFF. = 41%
*all figures are in millions of dollars

TABLE SEVEN

THE EXPLANATORY POWER OF THE GEOPOLITICAL POWER MODEL

PART ONE THE VALUE OF R SQUARED

INDICATORS		YEAR 68	69	70	71	72	73	74	75	76
TOTAL FOR MODEL	EX	XX	51	56	XX	50	64	65	75	53
	APP	39	56		55	48	54	60		44
	FFP									
POPULATION	EX	XX			XX		03		02	02
	APP		09				01@			01
	FFP									
MILITARY PER 1000 POPULATION	EX	XX	30	33	XX	28	42	32	50	19
	APP	37	67		52	42	44	54		21
	FFP									
LEVEL OF INTER-NATIONAL RESERVES	EX	XX	46	53	XX	39	54	23	66	42
	APP									38
	FFP									
MILITARY EXPENDITURES AS A % OF GNP	EX	XX			XX	48			75	
	APP		56							
	FFP									
GROSS SIZE OF MILITARY	EX	XX			XX					53
	APP									44@
	FFP									

blank = not significant XX = data not available
EX = Executive request APP = Congressional appropriations
FFP = Food For Peace funds @ = significant at the .1 level

TABLE SEVEN

THE EXPLANATORY POWER OF THE GEOPOLITICAL POWER MODEL

PART TWO THE VALUE OF THE UNSTANDARDIZED REGRESSION COEFFICIENT

INDICATORS		YEAR 68	69	70	71	72	73	74	75	76
POPULATION	EX	XX			XX	.41	.45		.59	.47
	APP		-.56				.27			.24
	FFP									
MILITARY PER 1000 POPULATION	EX	XX	.91	.58	XX	.96	.84	.45	1.1	.69
	APP	.50	.87		.52	.72	.52	.47		.40
	FFP									
LEVEL OF INTER-NATIONAL RESERVES	EX	XX	.88	.11	XX	.92	.85	.79	.28	.25
	APP									.18
	FFP									
MILITARY EXPENDITURES AS A % OF GNP	EX	XX			XX	-1.4			-.21	
	APP		-.19							
	FFP									
GROSS SIZE OF MILITARY	EX	XX			XX					.18
	APP									-.9
	FFP									
CONSTANT	EX	XX	1.44	1.5	XX	3.9	1.8	1.5	-.59	-.4
	APP	.43	.19		.84	.98	.70	.82		-.8
	FFP									

blank = not significant XX = data not available
EX = Executive request APP = Congressional appropriations
FFP = Food For Peace funds

TABLE EIGHT

THE EXPLANATORY POWER OF THE RECIPIENT NEED MODEL

PART ONE THE VALUE OF R SQUARED

INDICATORS		68	69	70	71	72	73	74	75	76
					YEAR					
TOTAL FOR MODEL	EX	XX	45	60	XX	43	40	42	50	27
	APP	37	38	23	61	39	34	56		36
	FFP	78								
PER CAPITA GNP	EX	XX	43	59	XX	38	40	40	50	
	APP	34	32	17	54	39	33	54		
	FFP									
BALANCE OF PAYMENT	EX	XX	11	16	XX				08	23
	APP				08					27@
	FFP	76								
INFANT MORTALITY	EX	XX			XX					
	APP				27					
	FFP									
LIFE EXPECTANCY	EX	XX			XX					
	APP									33@
	FFP									

blank = not significant XX = data not available
EX = Executive request APP = Congressional appropriations
FFP = Food For Peace funds @ = significant at the .1 level

TABLE EIGHT

THE EXPLANATORY POWER OF THE RECIPIENT NEED MODEL

PART TWO THE VALUE OF THE
UNSTANDARDIZED REGRESSION COEFFICIENT

INDICATORS		YEAR 68	69	70	71	72	73	74	75	76
PER CAPITA GNP	EX	XX	.26	.21	XX	.25	.26	.19	.36	
	APP	.21	.16	.20	.18	.19	.13	.18		
	FFP									
BALANCE OF PAYMENT	EX	XX	.79	.10	XX				.33	.34
	APP									.24
	FFP	.42								
INFANT MORTALITY	EX	XX			XX					
	APP				-.27					
	FFP									
LIFE EXPECTANCY	EX	XX			XX					
	APP									.12
	FFP									
CONSTANT	EX	XX	-1.2	1.5	XX	7.6	3.7	10.8	-.53	- 9
	APP	-.46	3.6	.87	6.3	5.8	7.1	5.1		-.5
	FFP	-1.6								

blank = not significant XX = data not available
EX = Executive request APP = Congressional appropriations
FFP = Food For Peace funds @ = significant at the .1 level

TABLE NINE

THE EXPLANATORY POWER OF THE STABILITY INTEREST MODEL

PART ONE THE VALUE OF R SQUARED

INDICATORS		YEAR 68	69	70	71	72	73	74	75	76
TOTAL FOR MODEL	EX	XX	35	43	XX	43	65	45	43	
	APP		38		50	38	39	57		
	FFP			35						
IRREGULAR EXECUTIVE TRANSFERER	EX	XX	33		XX					
	APP		24							
	FFP			10						
ARMED ATTACKS	EX	XX		43	XX	40	39	40	37	
	APP		62		49	38@	38	54		
	FFP			35						

blank = not significant XX = data not available
EX = Executive request APP = Congressional appropriations
FFP = Food For Peace funds @ = significant at the .1 level

TABLE NINE

THE EXPLANATORY POWER OF THE STABILITY INTEREST MODEL

PART TWO THE VALUE OF THE UNSTANDARDIZED REGRESSION COEFFICIENT

INDICATORS		YEAR 68	69	70	71	72	73	74	75	76
IRREGULAR EXECUTIVE TRANSFERER	EX	XX	2.4		XX					
	APP		2.7							
	FFP			11.9						
ARMED ATTACKS	EX	XX		.40	XX	.02	.37	.43	.15	
	APP		.17		.45	.01@	.21	.38		
	FFP			-.93						
CONSTANT	EX	XX	3.7	2.9	XX	4.6	4.2	3.6	4.3	
	APP		1.5		1.8	1.7	1.6	1.8		
	FFP			-2.1						

blank = not significant XX = data not available
EX = Executive request APP = Congressional appropriations
FFP = Food For Peace funds @ = significant at the .1 level

TABLE TEN

THE EXPLANATORY POWER OF THE SECOND POLITICAL IDEOLOGY INTEREST MODEL

PART ONE THE VALUE OF R SQUARED

INDICATORS		68	69	70	71	72	73	74	75	76
		YEAR								
TOTAL FOR MODEL	EX	XX		14@	XX	16@		23	17@	
	APP	16	14@					23		
	FFP									
ELECTIONS	EX	XX			XX			05@		
	APP	14					BS	03		
	FFP									
PROTEST DEMON-STRATIONS	EX	XX		14	XX	15			17	
	APP									
	FFP									
IMPOSITION OF POLITICAL SANCTIONS	EX	XX			XX			23	01	
	APP							23		
	FFP									
RELAXATION OF POLITICAL SANCTIONS	EX	XX			XX			11		
	APP							16		
	FFP									

blank = not significant XX = data not available
EX = Executive request APP = Congressional appropriations
FFP = Food For Peace funds @ = significant at the .1 level

TABLE TEN

THE EXPLANATORY POWER OF THE SECOND POLITICAL IDEOLOGY INTEREST MODEL

PART TWO THE VALUE OF THE UNSTANDARDIZED REGRESSION COEFFICIENT

INDICATORS		YEAR 68	69	70	71	72	73	74	75	76
ELECTIONS	EX	XX			XX			-3.1		
	APP	3.5						-2.5		
	FFP									
PROTEST DEMON- STRATIONS	EX	XX		-.6	XX	.69			1.3	
	APP									
	FFP									
IMPOSITION OF POLITICAL SANCTIONS	EX	XX			XX			-.37	-.82	
	APP							-.22		
	FFP									
RELAXATION OF POLITICAL SANCTIONS	EX	XX			XX			1.8		
	APP							1.4		
	FFP									
CONSTANT	EX	XX		2.3	XX	4.1		3.9	5.3	
	APP	1.1	XX					2.0		
	FFP									

blank = not significant XX = data not available
EX = Executive request APP = Congressional appropriations
FFP = Food For Peace funds @ = significant at the .1 level

TABLE ELEVEN

THE EXPLANATORY POWER OF THE FIRST SECURITY INTEREST MODEL

PART ONE THE VALUE OF R SQUARED

INDICATORS		YEAR 68	69	70	71	72	73	74	75	76
TOTAL FOR MODEL	EX	XX			XX	31@				
	APP	34	34			36				
	FFP		32	53	51			56	55	
U.S. * ARMS SALES	EX	XX			XX	05				
	APP	01@								
GROSS IMPORTS FROM U.S.S.R.	EX	XX			XX					
	APP		01							
	FFP			01	37					
U.S.* MILITARY .BASES	EX	XX			XX	28				
	APP	14	16			35				
U.S. DEFENSE TREATY	EX	XX			XX	20				
	APP	31	31			17				
	FFP								44	
NET EXPORTS TO USSR **		53	34@					50	03	
LEVEL OF COMMU-NSIT FOREIGN AID **				05	51					
USSR SECURITY INDEX**				49	12					

blank = not significant XX = data not available
EX = Executive request APP = Congressional appropriations
FFP = Food For Peace funds @ = significant at the .1 level
* = not significant for FFP
** = not significant for EX or APP all figures for FFP

TABLE ELEVEN

THE EXPLANATORY POWER OF THE FIRST SECURITY INTEREST MODEL

PART TWO THE VALUE OF THE UNSTANDARDIZED REGRESSION COEFFICIENT

INDICATORS		68	69	70	71	72	73	74	75	76
		YEAR								
U.S. * ARMS SALES	EX	XX			XX	-.50				
	APP	-.19								
GROSS IMPORTS FROM U.S.S.R.	EX	XX			XX					
	APP		-.38							
	FFP			-.13	-.30					
U.S. * MILITARY BASES	EX	XX			XX	4.7				
	APP	3.4	3.8			4.6				
U.S. DEFENSE TREATY	EX	XX			XX					
	APP	4.4	3.3			2.6				
	FFP								-2.7	
NET EXPORTS USSR **				.95	1.5		.51	.50		TO
LEVEL OF COMMUNSIT FOREIGN AID		**		.05	.51					
USSR SECURITY INDEX**				71.4	60.2					
CONSTANT	EX	XX			XX	4.9				
	APP	.52	.90			.63				
	FFP		.32	.69	2.3			1.2	-.27	

blank = not significant XX = data not available
EX = Executive request APP = Congressional appropriations
FFP = Food For Peace funds @ = significant at the .1 level * = not significant for FFP ** = not significant for EX or APP
all figures for FFP

TABLE TWELVE

THE EXPLANATORY POWER OF THE SECOND SECURITY INTEREST MODEL

PART ONE THE VALUE OF R SQUARED

INDICATORS		68	69	70	71	72	73	74	75	76
		YEAR								
TOTAL FOR MODEL	EX	XX	20@		XX					39
	APP	25@	20@							37
	FFP			52	33					
U.S. SECURITY INDEX	EX	XX	15		XX					
	APP	19	16							
	FFP			28@						
GROSS IMPORTS FROM U.S.S.R.	EX	XX			XX					
	APP	25@								
	FFP			35						
U.S.S.R SECURITY INDEX	EX	XX			XX					
	APP									
	FFP			27	31					
LEVEL OF COMMUNIST FOREIGN AID	EX	XX			XX					
	APP									
	FFP			-.51	-.32					

blank = not significant XX = data not available
EX = Executive request APP = Congressional appropriations
FFP = Food For Peace funds @ = significant at the .1 level

TABLE TWELVE

THE EXPLANATORY POWER OF THE SECOND SECURITY INTEREST MODEL

PART TWO THE VALUE OF THE UNSTANDARDIZED REGRESSION COEFFICIENT

INDICATORS		YEAR 68	69	70	71	72	73	74	75	76
U.S. SECURITY INDEX	EX	XX	7.3							
	APP	8.1	6.2							
	FFP			10.9						
GROSS IMPORTS FROM U.S.S.R.	EX	XX			XX					
	APP	-.39@								
	FFP			-.15						
U.S.S.R SECURITY INDEX	EX	XX			XX					
	APP									
	FFP			69.1	-2.5					
LEVEL OF COMMUNIST FOREIGN AID	EX	XX			XX					
	APP									
	FFP			-.51	-.32					
CONSTANT	EX	XX	2.2		XX					
	APP	.16	-.85							
	FFP			41.4	-1.7					

blank = not significant XX = data not available
EX = Executive request APP = Congressional appropriations
FFP = Food For Peace funds @ = significant at the .1 level

TABLE THIRTEEN

THE EXPLANATORY POWER OF THE ECONOMIC INTEREST MODEL

PART ONE THE VALUE OF R SQUARED

INDICATORS		68	69	70	71	72	73	74	75	76
TOTAL FOR MODEL	EX	XX								39
	APP									37
	FFP									
GROSS IMPORTS FROM U.S.	EX	XX			XX					02
	APP									01@
	FFP									
NET TOTAL INVESTMENT	EX	XX			XX					27
	APP									32
	FFP									
GROSS EXPORTS TO U.S.	EX	XX			XX					39
	APP									
	FFP									

blank = not significant XX = data not available
EX = Executive request APP = Congressional appropriations
FFP = Food For Peace funds @ = significant at the .1 level

TABLE THIRTEEN

THE EXPLANATORY POWER OF THE ECONOMIC INTEREST MODEL

PART TWO THE VALUE OF THE
UNSTANDARDIZED REGRESSION COEFFICIENT

INDICATORS		YEAR 68	69	70	71	72	73	74	75	76
GROSS IMPORTS FROM U.S.	EX	XX			XX					-.18
	APP									-.88@
	FFP									
NET TOTAL INVESTMENT	EX	XX			XX					.27
	APP									.23
	FFP									
GROSS EXPORTS TO U.S.	EX	XX			XX					.16
	APP									
	FFP									
CONSTANT	EX	XX			XX					1.6
	APP									1.0
	FFP									

blank = not significant XX = data not available
EX = Executive request APP = Congressional appropriations
FFP = Food For Peace funds @ = significant at the .1 level

TABLE FOURTEEN

THE EXPLANATORY POWER OF THE DEVELOPMENT INTEREST MODEL

PART ONE THE VALUE OF R SQUARED

INDICATORS		68	69	70	71	72	73	74	75	76
TOTAL FOR MODEL	EX	XX								38
	APP									57
	FFP		38	88	67					
PERCENT OF GNP IN MINING	EX	XX			XX					31@
	APP									45
	FFP									
PERCENT OF GNP IN AGRICULTURE	EX	XX			XX					25@
	APP									45
	FFP		37	88	67					

blank = not significant XX = data not available
EX = Executive request APP = Congressional appropriations
FFP = Food For Peace funds @ = significant at the .1 level

TABLE FOURTEEN

THE EXPLANATORY POWER OF THE DEVELOPMENT INTEREST MODEL

PART TWO THE VALUE OF THE UNSTANDARDIZED REGRESSION COEFFICIENT

INDICATORS		YEAR 68	69	70	71	72	73	74	75	76
PERCENT OF GNP IN MINING	EX	XX			XX					.23
	APP									.34
	FFP									
PERFECT OF GNP IN AGRICULTURE	EX	XX			XX					-.33
	APP									-.27
	FFP		-.69	.84	.87					
CONSTANT	EX	XX			XX					3.0
	APP									.55
	FFP		2.3	1.8	2.9					

blank = not significant XX = data not available
EX = Executive request APP = Congressional appropriations
FFP = Food For Peace funds @ = significant at the .1 level

TABLE FIFTEEN

THE EXPLANATORY POWER OF THE DOMESTIC INTEREST MODEL

PART ONE THE VALUE OF R SQUARED

DOMESTIC VARIABLES	REQUEST	APPROP.	FFP
	DEPENDENT VARIABLES		
UNEMPLOYMENT	NS	NS	NS
ECONOMIC AID AS A % OF TOTAL U.S. BUDGET	NS	NS	.01
GROSS VALUE OF U.S. FARM CROPS	NS	NS	.01
MULTILATERAL AID	NS	NS	.01
U.S. ELECTION YEAR	.01	NS	NS
CHANGE IN U.S. GNP	NS	NS	NS

NS = not significant

PART TWO

THE VALUE OF THE UNSTANDARDIZED REGRESSION COEFFICIENT

DOMESTIC VARIABLES	REQUEST	APPROP.	FFP
	DEPENDENT VARIABLES		
UNEMPLOYMENT	NS	NS	NS
ECONOMIC AID AS A % OF TOTAL U.S. BUDGET	NS	NS	.41
GROSS VALUE OF U.S. FARM CROPS	NS	NS	.24
MULTILATERAL AID	NS	NS	.08
U.S. ELECTION YEAR	.01	NS	NS
CHANGE IN U.S. GNP	NS	NS	NS

NS = not significant

TABLE SIXTEEN

THE EXPLANATORY POWER OF THE COMPOSITE MODEL

PART ONE THE VALUE OF R SQUARED

INDICATOR		YEAR 68	69	70	71	72	73	74	75	76
TOTAL FOR MODEL	EX	XX	62	32	XX	81	54	42	23	21
	APP	76	34	19	21	61	53	38	37	21
MILITARY PER 1000 POPULATION	EX	XX	54	56	XX	NS	63	57	71	41
	APP	61	69	NS	72	66	71	72	43	44
LEVEL OF INTER-NATIONAL RESERVES	EX	XX	67	72	XX	63	73	75	74	56
	APP	NS	NS	NS	NS	NS	NS	NS	NS	61
PER CAPITA GNP	EX	XX	41	68	XX	72	15	NS	NS	NS
	APP	65	NS	45	NS	13	72	02	NS	NS
ARMED ATTACKS	EX	XX	NS	31	XX	NS	43	23	NS	NS
	APP	NS	43	NS	76	NS	81	68	NS	NS

NS = not significant XX = data not available EX = Executive request APP = Congressional appropriations FFP = Food For Peace funds @ = significant at the .1 level

TABLE SIXTEEN

THE EXPLANATORY POWER OF THE COMPOSITE MODEL

PART TWO THE VALUE OF THE UNSTANDARDIZED REGRESSION COEFFICIENT

INDICATOR		YEAR 68	69	70	71	72	73	74	75	76
MILITARY PER 1000 POPULATION	EX	XX	.30	.14	XX	.31	.34	.18	.64	.32
	APP	.29	.29	NS	.27	.21	1.1	1.5	1.5	.22
LEVEL OF INTER-NATIONAL RESERVES	EX	XX	.87	1.1	XX	.95	.87	.79	NS	.82
	APP	NS	NS	NS	NS	NS	NS	NS	NS	1.9
PER CAPITA GNP	EX	XX	.80	.68	XX	.855	.54	NS	NS	NS
	APP	.12	NS	.20	NS	.53	.68	.13	NS	NS
ARMED ATTACKS	EX	XX	NS	1.9	XX	NS	1.0	1.3	NS	NS
	APP	NS	.71	NS	1.0	NS	.97	NS	NS	NS
CONSTANT	EX	2.2	2.4	.72	.90	1.2	2.1	1.6	1.1	.20
	APP	.24	.41	.40	.62	.60	.72	.38	.19	1.1

NS = not significant XX = data not available
EX = Executive request APP = Congressional appropriations
FFP = Food For Peace funds @ = significant at the .1 level

TABLE SEVENTEEN

PART ONE
THE SALIENCY OF THE INTERNATIONAL EXPLANATORY MODELS
AS MEASURED BY R SQUARED
FOR THE EXECUTIVE REQUEST FOR FUNDS

	YEAR						
MEASURES	69	70	72	73	74	75	76
GEO-POL.	S	S	S	S	S	S	S
REC. NEED	S	S	S	S	S	S	S
STABILITY	S	S	S	S	S	S	
2ND POL ID		S	S		S		
1ST SEC.			S				
2ND SEC.	S						
ECONOMIC							S
DEVELOPMENT							
1ST POL ID							

S = significant

TABLE SEVENTEEN

PART TWO
THE SALIENCY OF THE INTERNATIONAL EXPLANATORY MODELS
AS MEASURED BY R SQUARED
FOR THE CONGRESSIONAL APPROPRIATIONS

	YEAR								
MEASURES	68	69	70	71	72	73	74	75	76
GEO-POL.	S	S	S	S	S	S	S		S
REC. NEED	S	S	S	S	S	S	S		S
STABILITY		S		S	S	S	S		
1ST SEC.	S	S			S				
2ND SEC.	S	S							
2ND POL ID	S						S		
ECONOMIC									S
DEVELOPMENT									S
1ST POL ID									

S = significant

TABLE SEVENTEEN

PART THREE
THE SALIENCY OF THE INTERNATIONAL EXPLANATORY MODELS
AS MEASURED BY R SQUARED
FOR THE FOOD FOR PEACE PROGRAM

	YEAR								
MEASURES	68	69	70	71	72	73	74	75	76
1ST SEC.		S	S	S	S		S	S	
DEVELOPMENT		S	S	S					
2ND SEC.			S	S					
GEO-POL.	S								
REC. NEED	S								
STABILITY			S						
1ST POL ID									
2ND POL ID									
ECONOMIC									

S = significant

APPENDIX

RESEARCH NOTES

For the dependent variables a decision had to be made whether to operationalize the aid indicator as a gross measure, or to modify the indicator to reflect the relative size, of the recipient state's population and economy. A review of the aid measures adopted in the international literature proved inconclusive.

McKinlay and Little, in their 1977 article, adjusted the dependent variable to reflect both population and the recipient state's economy as measured by per capita GDP. However, in their 1979 article, unadjusted gross aid is operationalized as the dependent variable. (McKinlay and Little:77 & 79) Kato, whose research precedes McKinlay and Little's 1977 article by eight years, also uses the gross aid measure. (Kato:69)

Mosley, operationalized a different measure by adopting "aid as a percentage of recipient state GNP" for the dependent variable in the first stage of the two-staged least squares analysis. (Mosley:81) The four empirical studies used to guide this research have adopted three distinct measures to capture the level of foreign aid allocated to the recipient state by the donor state.

The question is whether there is theoretical justification for adjusting the dependent variable. And, if there is justification, should the dependent variable be adjusted to reflect population, the size of the recipient state's economy, or both? It is appropriate, in the opinion of this researcher, to adjust the dependent variable to reflect the population of the recipient state in an effort to reflect the variances in population and absorptive capacity across cases. However, adjusting the dependent variable to reflect the relative size of the recipient state's economy is rejected. McKinlay and Little's position that as "per capita GDP declines the relative need for aid rises" fails on two points. (McKinlay and Little:77:68)

First, the objective of the transformation is to adjust the dependent variable to reflect each recipient state's individual "relative need" for economic aid. While it is appropriate to measure the relative need of the recipient states according to the research design, the dependent variable ranks recipient states by measuring the level of foreign aid allocated by fiscal year. Any adjustment to the measure that reflects cross-state differences other than the level of aid should be operationalized as an independent variable.

It is more appropriate to operationalize the relative need concept as a independent variable, and complete the necessary tests to determine whether the relative need of the recipient state explains the allocation of foreign aid. The per capita GNP, and several other indicators, are operationalized to reflect the relative economic and human needs of the recipient states, and it is hypothesized that the level of foreign aid will reflect the relative needs of the recipient state. Transforming the dependent variable to reflect relative need violates the hypothesized causal sequence.

The second difficulty with an economic adjustment of the dependent variable is methodological. Several of the explanatory models operationalize indicators that are clearly related to the relative size of the recipient state's economy; included are per capita GDP, international liquidity, and the trade measures. Consequently, the transformation of gross aid to reflect the relative size of the recipient state's GDP or GNP increases the potential for simultaneous causation since both the dependent and independent variables contain measures effecting the recipient state's economy. The economic transformation of the level of aid compounds and increases this potential for simultaneous causation.

Mosley, in his analysis of the recipient need model, acknowledges the potential for simultaneous causation and takes corrective action. (see Chapter Two) However, Mosley limits his analysis to the recipient need model. In comparison this analysis operationalizes several models with indicators that measure different aspects of the recipient state's economy. Applying Mosley's correction procedure to these models and indicators presents several complex measurement and counting difficulties. It is more appropriate to avoid the problems of simultaneous causation by simply not adjusting the dependent variable to reflect the size of the recipient state's economy.

The transformation of the dependent variable to reflect the economy of the recipient state is rejected. However, McKinlay and Little's position that aid per capita, represents an appropriate transformation to reflect the relative size of the recipient state is accepted. (McKinlay and Little:77:67-69) Noting that the set of recipient states include India, with a population of some 700.5 millions, and Costa Rica with a population of 2.6 millions, it seems appropriate to adjust the dependent variable to reflect the relative size of the recipient state.

Also, as noted in Chapter Four, the variance in recipient state size increases the potential for a heterosedastic relationship between the error terms. The use of an unadjusted gross aid measure for the dependent variable increases this potential.

The comparative research literature raises serious questions concerning the reliability and consistency of per capita measures when using ordinary least squares. Fortunately, most of the concern is limited to those cases where per capita measures are operationalized as both dependent and independent variables. (Uslaner:76:125) Only one independent variable is operationalized as a per capita measure; per capita GDP.

Eric Uslaner, in his article "The Pitfalls of Per Capita" develops two decision rules to guide the researcher in the use of per capita measures; 1) where the interest of the researcher "involves explicit comparisons among cases . . . such as relative deprivation", and 2) where one has "prior knowledge that the relative independent variables actually employed by decision makers . . . includes standardized measures", such as per capita transformations. (Uslaner:76:132)

There are two questions in relation to the selection of per capita or gross aid measures that are pertinent to this research project. The first is whether the relative explanatory power of the models will vary depending on the selection of the foreign aid measure. The second question is whether the adoption of a per capita measure is justified by one or both of Uslaner's decision rules.

To address the first question, the dependent variables were operationalized as both per capita and gross levels of aid measures. The results for the recipient needs and geopolitical models are reported in Table Four. Generally, the explanatory power, as measured by R squared, was significantly greater, and in some cases substantially greater, for the gross aid measure in comparison to the per capita measure. In some cases, the explanatory power of the gross aid measure is more than twice the level than the per capita measure. However, in other cases recipient needs model 1968, a significant relationship was found for the per capita measure, but not for the gross aid measure. (see Table Four)

Appendix

Given the significance variance between the two measures of aid, the question becomes which is the most appropriate measure for this research project. Based on Uslaner's decision rules it appears that the per capita measure is more appropriate. To explain the allocation of bilateral foreign aid, it is necessary to measure the relative relationship between the donor and recipient state for each case. In effect providing for a comparison between cases, which is precisely the type of research situation referred to in Uslaner's first decision rule.

In reference to Uslaner's second decision rule, it appears appropriate to assume that foreign aid decision makers base some portion of their foreign aid allocation decisions on the per capita GDP of the recipient state. Per capita GDP, or per capita GNP, is commonly reported and used by both domestic and multilateral aid agencies as a means of classifying and determining the relative need of recipient states. In addition to the use of Uslaner's decision rules, the results of the per capita measures appear to be more reasonable in comparison to the gross aid measures. (see Table Four)

The question of per capita aid versus gross aid measures has been considered at some length because of the interesting methodological issues raised. It is clear that the adoption of one measure over the other will significantly affect the analysis of the causal relationship being tested. And, while the decision rules developed by Uslaner have aided in the selection of the per capita measure, the methodological cause of the variance across measures remains unknown. As a methodological question, explaining this variance has important implications and can improve our understanding of research methodology and foreign aid allocations.

The second research question pertains to the Executive request for funds. Unfortunately, the Executive request for Agency for International Development funds prior to fiscal year 1969 were classified and deleted from the Congressional records. Consequently, the data for fiscal year 1968 was not available through the Congressional sources used to collect the data. In addition, it was impossible to accurately measure the Executive request for fiscal year 1971.

As noted earlier, Agency for International Development expenditures are organized by activity categories, such as population and health. From fiscal year 1969 through 1976, the Executive branch organized its request by category of expenditure and recipient state. Consequently, it was necessary to add each category for each recipient state to determine the total Agency for International Development request per recipient state.

However, for 1971, the Executive budget request was by category with a description of planned activities for each recipient state. The level of foreign aid per recipient state by category was omitted. After considerable effort, it became quite clear that a consistent and reliable method of determining overall budget request per recipient state could not be developed from the Congressional sources utilized.

Why the Executive altered the form of its budgetary request for 1971 is unknown. However, 1971 was the height of the Vietnam War, and was a year of increasing Congressional opposition. Fiscal year 1971 was also the year that the Senate defeated the foreign aid bill, and Agency for International Development operated on continuing resolutions. Whether the Executive branch altered the format of its budgetary requests to hide Vietnam expenditures, or whether the Senate defeated the foreign aid bill in part because of the lack of clear, concise information is speculation. However, for fiscal year 1972, the Executive request reverted back to itemizing requested funds by category of expenditure and recipient state.

DATA SOURCES

ICPSR 7713 World Military Expenditures and Arms Transfers

ICPSR 7761 World Handbook of Social and Political Indicators III

ICPSR 7592 Cross-National Social-Economic Time Series

Political Handbook and Atlas of the World (Simon & Schuster)

Armed Forces of the World (sellers, Robert)

Statesman Yearbook

United Nations Demographic Yearbook, 1967-1976

United Nations Statistical Yearbook, 1967-1976

The Distribution of Financial Flows to Less Developed Countries (World Bank)

World Development Report, 1976-82 (World Bank)

Direction of Trade Flows, 1967-1976 (World Bank)

U.S. Overseas Loans and Grants, 1967-1976 (A.I.D.)

Report of the Senate Appropriations Sub-Committee on Foreign Assistance, 1967-1976

Report of the House Appropriations Sub-Committee on Foreign Assistance, 1967-1976

Harkavy, Robert, _Great Power Competition for Overseas Bases: The Geo-Politics of Access Diplomacy_, Pergamon Press, 1982

World Bank World Tables, 1976

U.S.S.R. Facts and Figures Annual 1977-1986, Academic International Press

A.I.D. Budget Submission to Congress, 1967-1976

BIBLIOGRAPHY

AID staff, "AID: Balancing critical Needs (US Proposal for Africa, Asia and Latin America), _Agenda_, published by AID, May 1982

Alston, Philip, "Human Rights and the New International Development Strategy", _Bulletin of Peace Proposals_, 1979, p.p. 280-290

Asher, Robert, _Development Assistance in the Seventies_, Brooking Institution, 1970

Asher, Robert, _Development Assistance in the D.D. II_, Brooking Institution, 1971

Black, Lloyd, _The Strategy of Foreign Aid_, D. Van Nostrand, 1968

Bollen, Kenneth, "Issues In The Comparative Measurement Of Political Democracy", _American Sociological Review_, June 1980, p.p. 370-390

Bollen, Kenneth, and Jackman, Robert, "Economic And Noneconomic Determinants Of Political Democracy In The 1960s", _Research In Political Sociology_, 1985, p.p. 27-48

Bollen, Kenneth, and Jackman, Robert, "Political Democracy And The Size Distribution Of Income", _American Sociological Review_, August 1985, p.p. 438-457

Bray, D.W., "President Carter's Human Rights Strategy", _CIO Press_, 1979

Brown, and Opie, _American Foreign Assistance_, Brooking Institution, 1953

Burns, James, _Presidential Government_, Houghton Mufflin, 1966

Carney, Kim, "Development Aid: An Economist's Perception", _International Journal On World Peace_, July-September, 1985, p.p. 3-35

Carrol, Holbert, _The House of Representatives and Foreign Affairs_, Little and Brown, 1966

Charlick, Robert B., "US And French Foreign Aid Rationale", _Public Policy_, 1965

Cohen, Benjamin, _American Foreign Economic Policy: Essays and Comments_, Harper and Row, 1968

Bibliography

Cohn, Steven, and Wood, Robert, "Basic Human Needs Programming: An Analysis of Peace Corp Data", Development and Change, Vol. 11, 1980, p.p. 313-332

Cohn, Steven, The Making Of United States International Economic Policy , second edition, Praeger, 1981

Cooper, Richard, "Economic Interdependence And Foreign Policy In The Seventies", paper presented at the Council Of Foreign Relations Conference On Trends Affecting International Relations, December, 1970

Clay, Lucius, D, Chairman of the, "The Committee To Strenthen The Security Of The Free World", The Scope And Distribution Of US Military and Economic Assistance Programs, Department of State, Publication, 1963

Cunningham, George, The Management of Aid Agencies, Croom Helm, 1974

Cutright, Phillips, and Wiley, James, "Modernization and Political Representation: 1927-1966", Studies In Comparative International Development, #5, 1969, p.p 23-66

Cutright, Phillips, "National Political Development", American Sociological Review, April 1973, p.p 253-264

Cutright, Phillips, "Inequality: A Cross - National Analysis", American Sociological Review, #32, 1967, p.p. 562-678

Davis, Otto, Dempster, M.A.H., and Wildavsky, Aaron, "Towards A Predictive Theory Of Governmental Expenditures: U.S. Domestic Appropriations", British Journal of Political Science, #4, 1974, p.p. 419-452

Downs, Anthony, Inside Bureaucracy, Little Brown, 1967

Deuth, Karl, W., The Analysis of International Relations, Prentice Hall, 1978

Fenno, Richard, Home Style House Members in Their Districts, Little Brown, 1978

Fenno, Richard, The United States Senate Bicameral Perspectives, American Enterprise Institute, 1982

Fenno, Richard, Congressmen In Committees, Little Brown, 1973

Fisher, Louis, The Politics of Shared Power Congress and the Executive, Congressional Quarterly Press, 1981

Bibliography

Frye, Alton, "Congress: The Virtue Of Its Vices", Foreign Policy, #3, Summer, 1971, p.p. 108-121

Geller, Daniel, "Economic Modernization And Political Instability In Latin America: A Causal Analysis Of Bureaucratic - Authoritarianism", Western Political Science Quarterly, March 1982, p.p. 33-49

General Assembly Sixth Special Session, the NIEO Resolutions, # 3201(s-vi), Declaration On The Establishment Of A New International Economic Order, and Resolution # 3202(s-vi), Program Of Action On The Establishment Of A New International Economic Order , 1974

Gist, John, Mandatory Expenditures And The Defense Sector: Theory Of Budgetary Incrementalism, Sage Publications, 1974

Goran, Ohlin, Foreign Aid Policies Reconsidered, OECD, 1966

Gordon, George, Public Administration In America, St. Martins, second edition, 1982

Goodell, G. "Conservatism And Foreign Aid", Policy Review, winter 1982, p.p. 111-131

Halpen, Morton, Bureaucratic Politics And Foreign Policy, Brooking Institution, 1974

Harsanyi, J.C., "Rational Choice Models Of Political Behavior vs. Functionalist and Conformist Theories", World Politics, July, 1969, 513-538

Hero, Alfred, "Foreign Aid And The American Public", Public Policy, March, 1965, p.p. 72-78

Hicks, Norman, and Streeten, Paul, "Indicators of Development: The Search for a Basic Needs Yardstick", World Development, vol. 7, 1979, p.p. 567-580

Hilsman, Roger, "Congressional - Executive Relations And The Foreign Policy Consensus", APSR , September, 1959

Hoadley, Stephen, "The Rise And Fall Of The Basic Needs Approach", Cooperation And Conflict, September, 1981

Holt, Pat, and Crabb, Cecil, Invitation To Struggle, Congress The President And Foreign Policy, second edition, Congressional Quarterly Press, 1984

Holsti, K.J., International Politics, Prentice Hall, forth edition, 1983.

Bibliography

Holt, Robert, and Richardson, John, "Competing Paradigms In Comparative Politics", Chapter two in Holt, Robert, and Turner, John, Methodology Of Comparative Research, The Free Press, 1976

Huntington, Samuel, Political Order In Changing Societies, Yale University Press, 1968

Huntington, Samuel, "Foreign Aid For What And For Whom", Foreign Policy, 1974.

Jackman, Robert, "Political Democracy And Social Equality: A Comparative Analysis", American Sociological Review, February, 1974, p.p. 29-45

Jackman, Robert, "On The Relation Of Economic Development To Democratic Performance", American Journal Of Political Science, vol. 17, 1973, p.p. 611-621

Jonsson, Christen, "The Ideology Of Foreign Policy", in Kegley, Charles, and McGowan, Pat, (editors), Foreign Policy USA/USSR, Sage Publication, 1982

Kato, Masakatsu, "A Model Of U.S. Foreign Aid Allocations: An Application Of A Rational Decision-Making Scheme", in Mueller, John (editor), Approaches To Measurement In International Relations, Appleton - Century - Crofts, 1969, p.p. 198-215

Katzenstein, Peter, "International Relations And Domestic Structures: Foreign Economic Policies Of Advanced Industrial States", International Organization, #30, winter, 1976, p.p. 1-46

Kegley, Charles, and Wittkopf, Eugener, World Politics Trends And Transformation, St Martins press, 1985

Kiewiet, Roderick, and McCubbins, Mathew, In The Mood: The Effect Of Election Year Considerations Upon the Appropriations Process, Paper prepared for delivery at the Annual Meeting of the Midwest Political Science Association, Cincinnati, Ohio, April 15-18, 1981

King, Gary, "How Not to Lie with Statistics: Avoiding Common Mistakes in Quantitative Political Science", American Sociological Review, July-August, 1986, p.p. 667-687

Koplan, Jacob, J., The Challenge Of Foreign Aid, Praeger, 1968

Bibliography

Kousoulas, D.G., *Power And Influence*, Brooks Cole, 1985

Legislative Reference Services Report, *US Foreign Aid*, Library of Congress, US Government Printing Office, 1969

Lindblom, C.E., *The Policy - Making Process*, Prentice Hall, 1968

Little, I.M.D., and Clifford, J.M., *International Aid*, Aldine Press, 1965

Little, Ian, M.D., *Economic Theory Policy And International Relations*, Basic Books, 1982

Liska G, *The New Statecraft: Foreign Aid In American Foreign Policy*, Chicago University Press, 1964

Liske, Craig, "Changing Patterns Of Partnership In Senate Voting On Defense And Foreign Policy 1947-69", in McGowan, Patrick, Editor, *Sage International Year Book Of Foreign Policy Studies: Volume III*, Sage Publications, 1975

Lowenthal, Abraham, F. "Foreign Aid As A Political Instrument: The Case Of The Dominican Republic", *Public Policy*, #14, 1965, p.p. 141-160

Mason, Edward, *Foreign Aid And Foreign Policy*, Harper and Row, 1964

McGowan, Pat, and Walker, Stephen, "Radical And Conventional Models Of US Foreign Economic Policy Making", *World Politics*, 81, p.p.347-382

McKinlay, R.D., and Little, R., "A Foreign Policy Model Of US Bilateral Aid Allocation", *World Politics*, October, 1977, 58-86

__________, and ____________, "The US Aid Relation ship: A Test of the Recipient Need And The Donor Interest Models", *Political Studies*, June 1979, 236-250

McLauchlin, (editor), *The United States And World Development Agenda*, Praeger, 1979

Morgan, E. Philip, "Social Analysis, Project Development And Advocacy In US Foreign Assistance", *Public Administration And Development*, January - March, 1983, p.p. 61-71

Montgomery, John, *The Politics Of Foreign Aid* , Praeger, 1962

Bibliography

Morgenthal, H.V., "A Political Theory Of Foreign Aid", American Political Science Review , #56, 1962

Morss, E. and Morss, L., US Foreign Aid, Westview, 1982

Mosley, Paul, "Models Of The Aid Allocation Process: A Comment On McKinlay And Little", Political Studies, June 1981, 245-253

Muhr, Lawrence, "The Concept Of Organizational Goal", American Political Science Review, June 1973, p.p. 470-481

Murray, Michael, Decisions a Comparative Critique, Pitman, 1986

Natchez, Peter, and Bupp, Irwin, "Policy And Priority In The Budgetary Process," American Political Science Review, #67, 1974, p.p. 951-963

Nelson, Joan, Aid: Influence And Foreign Policy, MacMillon, 1968

Ohiln, Gorain, Foreign Aid Policies Reconsidered, Development Center Studies, 1966

O'Leary, Michael, The Politics Of American Foreign Aid, Atherton, 1967

Packenham, Robert, Liberal America And The Third World: Political Development Ideas In Foreign Aid And Social Science, Princeton, 1973

Padget, John, "Bounded Rationality In Budgetary Theory", American Political Science Review, #74, 1980, p.p. 354-372

Palumbo, J. Dennis, Statistics In Political And Behavioral Science, Appleton-Century-Crofts, 1969

Pastor, Robert, Congress And The Politics Of US Foreign Economic Policy, University of California Press, 1980

Ripley, R., and Franklin, G., Congress The Bureaucracy And Public Policy, Dorsey Press, 1984

Rogowski, Ronold, "Rationalist Theories Of Politics: A Midterm Report", World Politics, January 1978, 296-323

Rosenna, James, "The Opinion - Policy Relationship" in Scott, Andrew, and Dawson, Raymond, (editors), Readings In The Making Of American Foreign Policy, 1965, p.p. 68-82

Bibliography

Rostow, W.W., "The Take-Off Into Self-Sustained Growth", The Economic Journal, March, 1956, p.p. 25-48

Rubinson,R. and Quinlan, "Democracy And Social Inequality: A Reanalysis", American Sociological Review, #42, 1977, p.p. 611-623

Schoultz, Lars, "US Foreign Policy And Human Rights Violations In Latin America", Comparative Politics, January, 1981, p.p. 149-170

Sharkansky, Ira, Public Administration, W. H. Freeman, 1982

Simon, Herbert, A., "A Behavioral Model Of Rational Choice", Quarterly Journal of Economics, Vol. #69 1955, 99-118

______________, Administrative Behavior: A Study of Decision Making Processes In Administrative Organizations, (3rd ed), The Free Press, 1976

Streeten, Paul, The Limits Of Development Research, Pergamon, 1975

Streeten, Paul, The Distinctive Features Of The Basic Needs Approach To Development, World Bank Basic Needs Papers #2, Washington, D.C., 1977

Tendler, Judith, Inside Foreign Aid, John Hoppkins University Press, 1975

Thorp, Willard, The Reality of Foreign Aid, Praeger, 1971

United Nations Conference For Least Developed Countries, Paris, September 1981, Pre-conference Documents, UN References #, A/CONF. 104/PC/14 (ADD.1), A/CONF.104/PC/19 (ADD. 2, 4, 5, &7), A/CONF.104/PC/13, A/CONF.104/2 (ADD.2), TD/RES/122(V):

United Nations Conference For Least Developed Countries, Paris, September 1981, "Informal Working Papers on the SNPA From Group B, Proposals Regarding the Structure of the Substantive New Programme of Action by the Chairman", UN References #, A/CONF. 104/PC/19/add. 5 and add.7

Uslaner, Eric, "The Pitfalls of Per Capita", American Journal of Political Science, February 1967, p.p. 125-133

Varshaey, Ashutosh, "Political Economy Of Western Aid To The Third World", India Quarterly, July-September, 1981, p.p.359-388

Bibliography

Waltz, Kenneth, _Theory Of International Politics_, Addison-Wesley Press, 1979

Wasserman, Cary, "The Foreign Aid Dilemma", _Washington Quarterly_, Winter, 1983, p.p. 96-106

Whale, Charles, Jr., _The House And Foreign Policy_, University of North Carolina Press, 1982

White, John, _The Politics Of Foreign Aid_, The Bodley Head, 1974

Wilcox, Francis, _The Congress The Executive And Foreign Policy_, Harper and Row, 1971

Wildavsky, Aaron, _The Politics Of The Budgetary Process_, Little Brown, fourth edition, 1984

Wittkopf, Eugene, "Western Bilateral Aid Allocations", _Sage International Studies Series_, #II, November, 5, 1972

Wood, Robert, "Foriegn Aid And The Capitalist State In Underdeveloped Countries", _Politics and Society_, #10, 1980, p.p. 1-34

For Product Safety Concerns and Information please contact our EU representative GPSR@taylorandfrancis.com
Taylor & Francis Verlag GmbH, Kaufingerstraße 24, 80331 München, Germany

www.ingramcontent.com/pod-product-compliance
Ingram Content Group UK Ltd.
Pitfield, Milton Keynes, MK11 3LW, UK
UKHW022219190926
475702UK00003B/440
* 9 7 8 0 3 6 7 3 4 8 7 8 6 *